Intercultural Communication

THE GERMANS AND THE ROMANIANS

EXPLAINED

ANDREEA SEPI

Copyright © 2016 - 2023 Andreea Sepi

All rights reserved.

LEGAL DISCLAIMER

CONTENTS

ACKNOWLEDGMENTS

The initial impulse for writing this book can be found in my own efforts at cultural adjustment following my immigration from Romania to Germany, as well as in Romania's subsequent European integration in 2007. Seven years later, in 2014, all restrictions on the free circulation of Romanian laborers in the EU were dropped. While this did not immediately result in the much-feared "exodus" of Romanians towards the more prosperous EU states, it has contributed to a gradual but steady flow of Romanian workers to Germany – a situation that prompted a closer look at both cultures, their interactions, and their potential for collaboration. This book aims to serve as a guide for cross-cultural interactions in the business and private sphere and can be a useful tool in cross-cultural management.

I thank my family for putting up with my obsessions, the Germans for putting up with me, Adina Tuner and Roxana Albu for their useful comments and suggestions, and Prof. Dr. Ulrike A. Kaunzner and Prof. Dr. Brigitte Teuchert from the University of Regensburg for their positive feedback.

Like shampoo and conditioner, this book is **2 in 1**. It is a comparative study of German and Romanian attitudes, behaviors, and communication patterns. It looks at the German and Romanian cultures through three lenses: that of reliable international models, that of national research and self-image, and that of mutual hetero-comparison to derive valid cultural profiles. It then shows how these profiles are reflected in language, sayings, set phrases, idiomatic expressions, folklore, humor, communication style, and practices – and goes on to offer suggestions for improved mutual understanding.

This book represents self-published research. I apologize in advance for any possible errors, omissions, or inconsistencies.

1. ICC – Inter*what*…???

Western Romania. I am entering a fashion store to look at some jackets. A smiling shopkeeper (I can only see her eyes above the mask, but I can tell she is smiling) immediately approaches me, notices the items I am exploring, and tells me what a good choice I have made. She then proceeds to tell me she has a jacket just like the ones I am interested in and that she is more than happy with it. She lists some of the benefits, counters all my objections boldly, and entices me with a discount, which she immediately confirms with her boss by picking up the phone and sending a text. Within minutes, she has closed the deal, and I am leaving the store a happy customer, pleased with my new purchase.

Now, make no mistake about it. Not all Romanian shopkeepers are this pro-active or friendly. Not by a long shot. That is not the point. But this one knew exactly what I, as a Romanian customer, was likely to react positively to.

Rewind to Upper Bavaria, a couple of years before the pandemic. I've been sick for a week and I'm entering the pharmacy to get some vitamin gummy bears and maybe a nose spray.

The only shop assistant present is busy going through the entire cosmetics product range with a middle-aged woman. He does not look up or say hello. I feel invisible.

Besides me, there is another lady with a seven-year-old kid, looking undecided. I start to sweat under my shawl, waiting. Eventually, a second shop assistant (male) appears. I let the lady with the kid go first, even though I was already clutching my gummy bears and I was sweating through every pore.

And then I wait.

She had ordered a silicone nipple for a baby bottle the other day and is here to pick it up. The guy brings her 4 different versions. She realizes she doesn't know which one (if any!) will match the plastic ring for the bottles she has at home. The shop assistant launches a thorough database search and comes up with 225 different types of plastic rings he could procure (yes, no kidding, actual number). He gets briefly interrupted by a dog (his pet), escaped from the back office (again, all true!)

In the meantime, four more people, all of them seniors, have entered the pharmacy and are waiting in line looking tense. The first shop assistant is still describing facial treatments, oblivious of the rest. She completely avoids eye contact. Nobody seems to notice the five drained customers standing like five white elephants in the middle of a very cramped store. The woman with the feeding bottles is still undecided, the shop assistant moves in fastidious slow motion, letting her spill all her beans, catering to her drawling indecision. Now he's giving his opinion on which supplier is more trustworthy and willing to accommodate different combinations.

What is going on here?

If you've ever been in that situation, or think you might find yourself in one soon enough, this book is for you. It attempts to clarify differences and dispel misperceptions that still endure on both sides of an intercultural encounter – or, should I say, on both sides of a cultural divide. Learning to communicate better across cultures can (hopefully!) contribute to minimizing misunderstandings and tensions in the context of family, business negotiations, or public services and policies. This book's purpose is to analyze and compare the German and Romanian cultures using a combination of approaches from social science, management science, cultural studies/anthropology, psychology, and linguistics. It maps the two cultures based on the most commonly used models in intercultural communication and attempts a comparative synthesis.

As demonstrated by numerous experiments in social psychology (Pondy 1967), conflict among people usually arises out of differences of perception and interpretation of the same event, situation, or gesture (cognition) – and subsequently grows through emotionalization.

Psychology also shows that self-suggestion or even a small change in the perception angle can lead to dramatically altered interpretations of what is being seen or experienced.[1] In turn, distorted perceptions and interpretations can lead to social contagion and a loss of empathy, making it possible to go from slight personal irritation to all-out conflict.

---

[1] Lassiter, G.D. et al., "Attributional Complexity and the Camera Perspective Bias in Videotaped Confessions" in BASIC AND APPLIED SOCIAL PSYCHOLOGY, 27(1), 2005, pp. 27–35

It thus stands to reason that an important (and often ignored) filter such as culture, which permeates and influences most of our daily perceptions and interpretations, can pose quite a challenge in our increasingly global society. The goal of this book is to raise awareness about our social programming, dismantle prejudice, and challenge this mutual ignorance.

Intercultural communication (ICC), intensified and accelerated by the increasing globalization of our world following WWII and the ensuing liberalization of trade in some parts of the world, can be defined as the process and form of communicating across cultures: an attempt at understanding how people from different cultures, backgrounds, and countries interact, communicate, and perceive or appraise reality. Over the past 50 years, ICC has developed into a fully-fledged science, with methods, theories, models, and best practices. Wikipedia, for instance, defines Intercultural Communication as "a form of communication that aims to share information across different cultures and social groups. It is used to describe the wide range of communication processes and problems that naturally appear within an organization or social context made up of individuals from different religious, social, ethnic, and educational backgrounds."

So, if *inter*cultural communication is the process of exchanging and interpreting information between people of different cultures, it then follows that the essential issue we need to define in order to better understand the art and science of intercultural communication is that of *culture* itself. But what *is* culture?

1.1. Definitions, components, and characteristics of culture

If we are to believe anthropologist E. T. Hall (1990), culture is communication. UNESCO (2001) defines culture as "the set of distinctive spiritual, material, intellectual and emotional features of society or a social group, that encompasses not only art and literature but lifestyles, ways of living together, value systems, traditions, and beliefs".

There are many definitions of culture and as such, many metaphors of culture. Culture as an iceberg, culture as social and psychological programming, culture as islands in an ocean, culture as a filter or a screen are a few that come to mind[2]. For the founding father of intercultural communication, "the world of communication can be divided into three parts: words, material things, and behavior"[3].

E. B. Tylor (1871), considered by many the originator of cultural anthropology, wrote: "Culture, or civilization, taken in its broad, ethnographic sense, is that complex whole which includes knowledge, belief, art, morals, law, custom, and any other capabilities and habits acquired by man as a member of society".[4] About a century later, anthropologist James Spradley[5] defined culture as the "knowledge that is learned and shared and that people use to generate behavior and interpret experience". Put succinctly, then, culture is a

---

[2] See also, www.culture-at-work.com, 06.06.2016
[3] Hall, E. T., Hall M. R., *Understanding Cultural Differences*, Intercultural Press Inc., Yarmouth, 1990, p.3
[4] Tylor, E. B., *Primitive Culture*, J.P. Putnam's Sons, New York, 1920 (1871), vol. 1, p.1
[5] McCurdy, D. W., Spradley, J., Shandy, D. J., *The Cultural Experience - Ethnography in Complex Society*, Second Ed., Waveland Press, Long Grove, 2005, p. 5

system of learned patterns for configuring, interpreting, making sense of, and relating to the world – and there are many types of cultures and subcultures.

The English Thesaurus dictionary defines culture in its anthropological sense as "the sum total of ways of living built up by a group of human beings and transmitted from one generation to another."

I define culture as the shared worldview, mindset, and behaviors of a particular community of human beings, obtained primarily through socialization – i.e. all their shared beliefs, values, attitudes, norms, behaviors, and artifacts. To put it briefly, culture means "how we interpret and do things around here".

For this book, I have explored culture at a national level – that is, the way of living, communicating, understanding reality, and doing things typical of the people who are born, raised, and who live within the state borders of a particular country. Of course countries today are not, nor have they ever been, fully homogeneous. There are subcultures and co-cultures within each, just as there are a variety of organizational or family cultures, personal inclinations, etc. But for the purposes of simplifying the area of our research, I shall attempt to identify an encompassing cultural pattern at the national level. In other words, our definition of culture shall be that of 'national' or 'ethnic' culture.

Going back to the iceberg metaphor of culture – if you care to join me on this fascinating ride – we are going to investigate the cognitive, emotional, and linguistic levels (or substrata) of the observable (behavioral) tip of the iceberg for the contemporary German and Romanian cultures. And, like E. T. Hall, we are concerned with ways to translate behavior from one culture into another.

Any culture has several components and characteristics. Whether adaptive or symbolic or both, it is a system of collective values, beliefs, norms, behaviors, and behavioral patterns that help generate cohesion within a larger group of people, help them work with and adjust to the environment, and are transmitted during the individuals' socialization process. As such, it is complex (sometimes contradictory), situational, learned, and dynamic; although it does usually exhibit great inertia in the face of change.

Towards the end, we will also have a look at how values are reflected in communication and linguistic patterns in both German and Romanian.

Of course, culture is a living organism. It evolves. New political systems, membership in transnational organizations (such as the EU), access to international pop culture, new technologies, globalization, and new business models engender new ways of doing and thinking about things, as well as more uniform patterns of behavior. Our representation of cultural profiles is merely a snapshot taken at a particular point in time. We have to rely on some degree of generalization if we are to deliver results that have any practical use whatsoever. However, one should remain aware that our results are only general tendencies, statistically relevant occurrences; by no means do they claim to represent some kind of absolute, unanimous truth.

1.2. History and theories of ICC

Beginning at the end of the 19th century, with the first truly international companies, and continuing with the trade liberalization in the Western world after the Second World War, many businesses stopped being local undertakings and instead became increasingly global. Technological advances, the advent of the Internet and other mobile technologies, the integration of markets etc. have made it possible to run a business across continents, extracting the raw material from one country, manufacturing products in another, coordinating and developing strategies in yet another, and selling practically everywhere. Increased migration of the workforce and business networks that stretch across the globe have created a need for better and more effective intercultural communication – to integrate immigrants, to lead employees, to reach financial targets, to drive sales. People need to be understood and talked to "in their own language". Whether exporting goods, manufacturing them in a foreign country, or importing workforce, businesses and governments need to understand different cultural contexts, how they are perceived, and how people do things elsewhere.

French anthropologist and ethnologist Claude Levi Strauss had already introduced the notion and the exigency of cultural relativism (which affirms that no culture has absolute criteria for judging another as low or as noble, but it can and should evaluate itself) thus clearing the way for some formidable achievements in the field of intercultural communication.

Starting in the 1960s, especially in the English-speaking world, scientists such as Kluckhohn & Strodtbeck, E. T. Hall, G. Hofstede, F. Trompenaars, Richard D. Lewis, or Thomas Alexander in the German space, have begun to delve deeper into the subjects of culture and intercultural communication, developing several theories that have enjoyed great traction.

The first to use the actual term "intercultural communication" in his research was E.T. Hall (1959), who is rightfully considered the founding father of intercultural communication (ICC) as an academic field of study. His research influenced much of the work on culture and intercultural communication done throughout the 1960s and 1970s and his approach continued to be acknowledged throughout the 1990s. C. Kluckhohn, F. Kluckhohn and F. L. Strodtbeck (Culture and Behavior - 1962, Variations in Value Orientations - 1961) were also a large influence. The field of intercultural communication positively flourished during the 1980s and 1990s with the work of G. Hofstede and Trompenaars and under the hegemonic influence of quantitative methodologies. In the 1990s, the journal "International and Intercultural Communication Annual" began to promote the use of qualitative methodology as well.

Today, social, cultural, and intercultural psychology all study the way culture (norms, values, social institutions) and relationships in and among groups of people shape the way we act and behave. The 45th Division of the American Psychological Association is called the Society for the Psychological Study of Culture, Ethnicity and Race and issues the Cultural Diversity and Ethnic Minority Psychology Review. The International Association for Cross-Cultural Psychology was founded in 1972 and publishes the prestigious Journal of Cross-Cultural Psychology.

The discipline of ethnic or national psychology originates in the German environment, where the first structured and programmatic attempts at identifying the psychological attributes of nations and peoples appeared in the 19th century, under the name *Völkerpsychologie*. This term was introduced by Moritz Lazarus and Heymann Steinthal (1851, 1859), who were influenced by Hegelian philosophy and logic. They argued that a group of people is more than the sum of its individual members, that it possesses a common ethos or spirit (a *Volksgeist*) and generates cultural products and responses that cannot be reduced to the sum of individual responses or products. Their concept received heavy criticism later on as the definition of this "ethos" was vague, unclear, and used to explain rather than to simply describe behavior, thus reversing the scientific causality. In 1886, Wilhelm Wundt of the University of Leipzig gives new meaning to the term *Völkerpsychologie*, seeking to avoid the controversial ethos theory and to do a comparative research of language and cultural practices of more people, with empirical and phenomenological methodology.[6] His efforts were also criticized and failed to win much recognition in the long term.

More recently, a team of researchers from the University of Regensburg around A. Thomas and S. Schroll-Machl have put together an important body of research on German cultural standards and intercultural communication. In *Handbuch Interkulturelle Kommunikation und Kooperation* (2003), Sylvia Schroll-Machl describes communication as "the most important form of social interaction" and sees the overlapping and intersection of cultures as playing a crucial and central role that affects the means of communication, the channels of communication (acoustic, optic, tactile, interpersonal, and mediated), the

---

[6] David, D., *Psihologia poporului român*, Ed. Polirom, Bucharest, 2015, p.30

relationships in a communication (symmetrical or asymmetrical), and the functions of communication (according to Schulz von Thun the four "sides" of every message: factual relaying of information, relationship-building, self-revelation, and persuasion or influence).[7]

In Romania, sociologist and ethnologist Dimitrie Gusti (1880-1955) wrote about social units and culture as "social will", showing that the latter is conditioned by cosmic, biological, psychological, and historical factors. Constantin Rădulescu-Motru (1868-1957), a reputed sociologist, psychologist, philosopher, and member of the Romanian Academy, developed the concept of *Romanianism*, supporting cultural and national dialogue instead of isolation in ethnicity. Building on Wundt's *Völkerpsychologie* (in whose laboratory at the University of Leipzig he worked and studied), but adding his original contributions, he attempted to assess and define nationalism in the Romanian social context, with a focus on adapting modern Western forms to the Romanian ethnicity which he perceived as a true social foundation. Perhaps his most notorious contribution to the field of ethnic social psychology is his 1910 book, *Sufletul neamului nostru. Calități bune și defecte* ("The spirit of our nation. Its good qualities and its flaws").

In 2015, psychology professor Dr. Daniel David of the University of Cluj-Napoca, Romania, published a very complex and detailed book called *Psihologia poporului român - Profilul psihologic al românilor într-o monografie cognitiv-experimentală* ("The Psychology of the Romanian People - The

---

[7] Thomas, A., Kammhuber, S., Schroll-Machl, S., *Handbuch Interkulturelle Kommunikation und Kooperation*, Vandenhoeck& Ruprecht, Göttingen, 2003, p.102

Psychological Profile of Romanians in a Cognitive-Experimental Monograph"), which investigates culture as a combination of superficial and deep traits, attempting to outline the specific psychological profile of Romanians using self- and hetero-comparison, as well as national and international research with statistically significant samples.

An explanatory narrative of why Romania is often seen as different or "exocentric" from the European average or from Western norms was delivered by historian Lucian Boia (2012). His book *De ce este România altfel?* ("Why is Romania different?") brings to light the geopolitical and historical context in which Romanians evolved as a nation and its peculiarities to show why and how some of the more "typical" Romanian cultural traits emerged.

2. Analyzing Cultures: I Love Diagrams!

2.1. Authors, models, and dimensions of culture. Germany and Romania according to each model

2.1.1. E. T. Hall's groundbreaking work

Edward Twitchell Hall (1914-2009), an American anthropologist, is credited with having established the field of intercultural communication as a scientific discipline within the realm of anthropology. He taught at several world-renowned universities in the United States, such as the University of Denver, Harvard Business School, Illinois Institute of Technology, and Northwestern University.

In the 1930s he lived with the Navajo and Hopi populations in Arizona, investigating their culture. After receiving his Ph.D. in Anthropology from Columbia University in 1942, he went on to study and experience culture in Europe, the Middle East, and Asia. During the Second World War, he served in Europe and the Philippines. His experiences led him to what would become his central topic of research. He became convinced that misunderstandings between cultures occur because of a specific yet universal matrix of parameters. During the 1950s he worked for the U.S. State Department, at the Foreign Service Institute, where he taught intercultural communication skills to foreign service personnel. During his career, Hall coined several important concepts in the academic field of intercultural communication, such as: "high-context culture", "low-context culture", "proxemics", "polychronic time", "monochronic time", which can be applied as a framework for comparing and understanding cultures "by revealing the underlying patterns of behavior"[8].

Hall's work was groundbreaking, opening up an entirely new field of research. Some of his most substantial influences have been the introduction of **nonverbal aspects** of communication, specifically proxemics, the study of the social uses of space, to the investigation of communication between members of different cultures.

In E. T. Hall's view, cultures differ in terms of informational **context** (low or high), **attitude towards time** (monochronic vs. polychronic), and **use of space** (proxemics).

In Hall's own words (1976), "a high context (HC) communication or message is one in which most of the information is already in the person, while very little is in the coded, explicit, transmitted part of the message. A low-context (LC) communication is just the opposite; i.e. the mass of the information is vested in the explicit code."

According to Hall, in **high-context cultures,** messages are not fully explicit. One needs to rely on context (inferred, indirect, implicit information) to make sense of them. This means that people understand the rules through the many contextual elements that exist and a good level of understanding depends on good knowledge of the context. Thus, the rules are often unwritten and people unfamiliar with the culture can find it very confusing to navigate; whereas those familiar with the culture take these rules for granted and may not even

---

[8] E. T. Hall, M. R. Hall, *Understanding Cultural Differences*, Intercultural Press Inc., Yarmouth, 1990, p.xix

be consciously aware of them. One typical example is France. Romania is another.

In a **low-context culture**, on the other hand, communication is very explicit. No one takes the rules for granted, they are typically set out and explained in detail, thus avoiding confusion. Extensive and detailed previous knowledge of the cultural context is not absolutely necessary to understanding. Examples of low-context cultures are the United States of America and, of course, Germany.

But how do cultures differ in their perception of time? In high-context cultures, time is flexible. Objectives are achieved (eventually) but not necessarily in a highly organized way, and the process is more important than the outcome. These cultures are **polychronic**, meaning their members work on different tasks simultaneously and are convinced that they get more done this way. Polychronic people do several things at once, with many interruptions. They are committed to people and to human relationships and change plans often and easily to accommodate other people or life events. They also borrow and lend things often and easily and tend to build lifelong relationships.

By contrast, in low-context cultures time tends to be **monochronic** – doing one thing at a time, with careful planning and scheduling, is the rule. People tend to be very organized, with a focus on rigorous time management and punctuality – members of such cultures believe that serial mono-tasking is more likely to get them quality results; furthermore, the outcome is more important than the process of achieving it. They are committed to promptness, punctuality, they tend to focus on the job/result rather than on people, show great respect for private property, seldom lend or borrow and adhere religiously to plans and privacy norms.

2.1.1.1. Germany vs. Romania in E.T. Hall's model

A comparison between Germany and Romania along Hall's cultural parameters will quickly reveal two very different (almost completely opposed) ways of doing things. While the Germans are usually low-context and monochronic, expressing everything clearly and directly and favoring mono-tasking, Romania, given its Latin character, is high-context and polychronic. Germans need a wider personal space than Romanians do; the latter use a lot more touching and their space is also more 'disorganized' (see table).

Parameter/Culture	Context	Time	Space
Germany	Low-context	Monochronic	Distance, privacy
Romania	High-context	Polychronic	Closeness, openness

Table 1. Germany vs. Romania in E.T. Hall's model[9]

It can be easily seen that the two cultures are at odds with each other in every dimension, which creates fertile ground for cultural misunderstanding leading to mutual prejudice.

---

[9] Note: the characteristics for German culture stem from Hall, E. T. and Hall, M.R, *Understanding Cultural Differences - Germans, French and Americans*, Intercultural Press Inc., Yarmouth, 1990, pp 33-83. (The evidence for Romania comes from my lifelong experience as a native Romanian and that of observers I have had conversations with.)

The interviews Hall conducted in Germany for his book (mostly in large urban and business centers in Northern Germany) indicate that German culture exhibits most clearly the following characteristics:

- precise scheduling and slow pace

- inviolate private space

- doors as barriers

- intellectual power (academic degree) ranks very high

- order, great respect for norms and procedures, conformity

- efficiency, authority, and control

- inflexibility

- extreme compartmentalization (of time, space, work)

- possessions are important and treated meticulously

- formal communication based on politeness and distance, directness, convoluted phrases, exactness of language, earnestness

- written communication is preferred.

Many of these characteristics are completely reversed in Romanian culture. With their Latin roots, Orthodox religion, Slavic/Oriental/Balkan, and later French influences, their troubled history, and difficult geostrategic position, Romanians traditionally exhibit a much laxer sense of time, personal space, and commitment to worldly values such as material possessions.

Romanian culture favors:

- flexible scheduling, doing several things at once

- smaller personal space and a much more diffuse separation between home and work, private and public; informal networks are important
- academic achievement is still important on paper and for prestige, but money, connections, and position in the hierarchy matter more
- distrust of state authority, a hidden desire not to conform, reluctance to be hemmed in by non-negotiable rules
- flexibility in thought, extreme dislike for dogmatism and rigidity
- creativity, innovation, and improvisation
- pragmatism and opportunism
- possessions are becoming more and more important as status symbols and there is increasing competition for "the best" goods and positions
- traditionally, people part more easily with money and objects, sharing is encouraged from a young age (but this is also changing: spending and tipping now a marker of prosperity)
- formal communication based on politeness, but also reaching familiarity and friendliness relatively quickly; understanding the general idea or the outline of something is often considered enough, we will figure out the rest as we go along
- spoken communication (picking up the telephone rather than writing an e-mail).

2.1.2. A true heavyweight. Cultural dimensions according to G. Hofstede

Geert Hofstede is a Dutch social psychologist and Professor Emeritus of Organizational Anthropology and International Management at Maastricht University in the Netherlands. He is best known for his pioneering work on cross-cultural organizations. His research and subsequent model of cultural dimensions became the resource of choice for expats, international management experts, CEOs, and trainers the world over.

As he claims in the preface to the first edition of *Cultures and Organizations - Software of the Mind* (1991, McGraw-Hill), his interest in cultural differences happened accidentally in the late 1960s. His access to rich data for studying them resulted in the publication in 1980 of his book *Culture's Consequences*. The book met with great interest at the time and was later reformulated using extensive empirical research and a rigorous quantitative methodology.

Geert Hofstede's point of view is that of "culture as mental programming"[10]. His tenet is that culture is learned, not inherited. This process starts with socialization in childhood but continues throughout a lifetime. Thus, culture might be described as a kind of "software of the mind" – patterns of thinking, feeling, and behaving which are engrained in our being. We can deviate from them, but that often proves difficult as they are hard-wired through the repeated influence (and pressure) of the environment. And since culture is a collective phenomenon, so Hofstede believes culture can be

---

[10] Hofstede, G., *Cultures and Organizations - Software of the Mind*, McGraw-Hill, New York, 1997, p.4

portrayed as "a collective programming of the mind which distinguishes the members of one group or category of people from another"[11].

According to Hofstede (1991), at the core of each culture there are values, rituals, heroes and symbols, and lastly, permeating through them all, as the most concrete manifestation of culture – practices. In his view, for organizational and business purposes one can best describe and analyze a culture using the following cultural dimensions:

The **Power Distance Index (PDI)** describes power distribution and the extent to which the less powerful members of organizations and institutions (including the family) accept and expect that power is distributed unequally. This represents inequality but defined from below. It suggests that a society's level of inequality is endorsed by the followers as much as by the leaders. Power and inequality are fundamental facts of any society, so "all societies are unequal, but some are more unequal than others".

Individualism (IDV) versus its opposite, **collectivism**, is the degree to which individuals are integrated into groups and the measure of how tight these ties are. In individualist societies the ties between individuals are loose: everyone is expected to look after him/herself and his/her immediate family. Collectivist societies are those in which people are integrated from birth into strong, cohesive in-groups, who take care of each other – often extended families (with uncles, aunts, and grandparents) defined by unquestioning loyalty. The word 'collectivism' in this sense has no political meaning for Hofstede: it refers to the

---

[11] Hofstede, G., *Cultures and Organizations - Software of the Mind*, McGraw-Hill, New York, 1997, p.5

group, not the state. Again, the issue addressed by this dimension is an extremely fundamental one, regarding all societies in the world.

Masculinity (MAS) versus **femininity** refers to a success-driven society versus a quality-of-life-driven society, as well as the distribution of roles between the genders. Hofstede's IBM studies revealed that (a) women's values differ less among societies than men's values; (b) men's values can range from very assertive and competitive and maximally different from women's in some societies, to modest and caring and very similar to women's in others. The assertive pole has been called 'masculine' and the modest, more caring pole 'feminine'.

The **Uncertainty Avoidance Index (UAI)** deals with a society's tolerance for uncertainty and ambiguity. It indicates to what extent a culture 'teaches' its members to feel either uncomfortable or comfortable in situations that are novel, unknown, surprising, different from usual. Uncertainty avoiding cultures try to minimize the possibility of such unstructured situations by strict laws and rules, safety and security measures and networks, or – on a philosophical and religious level – through faith, a belief in absolute Truth, traditions, and rituals. People in uncertainty-avoiding countries are often more emotional and motivated by inner nervous energy. The opposite type, uncertainty accepting cultures, are more tolerant of different opinions and ways of doing things; they try to have as few rules as possible and, on the philosophical and religious level, they are relativistic and allow many currents to flow side by side.

Long-Term Orientation (LTO) versus Short-Term Orientation: this fifth dimension was found in a study on students from 23 countries around the world, using a questionnaire designed by Chinese scholars. Values associated with long-term orientation are thrift and perseverance; values associated with short-term orientation are: respect for tradition, fulfilling social obligations, and protecting one's 'face'. Both the positively and the negatively rated values of this dimension are found in the teachings of Confucius, the most influential Chinese philosopher who lived around 500 B.C.; however, according to Hofstede, the dimension also applies to countries without a Confucian heritage.

Recently, Geert Hofstede and his team of researchers have added yet another dimension to their analysis of cultures. This is **Indulgence vs. Restraint (IvR)**: the extent to which people try to control their desires and impulses based on the way they were raised and social constraints. Relatively weak control is called "indulgence" and relatively strong control is called "restraint". Cultures can, therefore, be described as indulgent or restrained.

2.1.2.1. Germany vs. Romania in G. Hofstede's model

How do Romania and Germany fare in Hofstede's model, and what are their major differences or similarities? This can easily be seen if we compare them using the software on Hofstede's website (2016). For the purposes of this book, however, I have also drawn on Hofstede (1997), Hofstede et al. (2010), as well as on a detailed study on Romanian cultural dimensions, management practices, and preferences by Interact Romania (2005).

Stressing, as Hofstede does, that these dimensions are only constructs that do not exist in reality, and are only useful to infer certain traits about a culture, here are the results of Hofstede's estimates about Romania and Germany, with the areas of relative similarity represented in gray:

Parameter/ Culture	PDI	IDV	MAS	UAI	LTO	IvR
Germany	Low PDI 35	Individualistic 67	Masculine 66	High UA 65	Long-term orientation 83	(relatively) Restrained 40
Romania	High PDI 90	Collectivistic 30	Feminine (relative) 42	High UA 90	Intermediate orientation 52	Restrained 20

Table 2. Germany vs. Romania in G. Hofstede's model[12]

In other words, Hofstede's research shows that while Germans are more individualistic and driven by achievement, define themselves through their work, have a flatter distribution of power in society, and think in the long term while exercising a relative degree of internalized restraint (thrift, savings, avoiding waste), Romanians are more collectivistic, pragmatic, and short-term oriented, 'working to live' (not living to work), and very restrained (tendency towards pessimism and distrust, like 'what's the use', 'our turn will never come' or 'it's too good to be true'). Although they are often in competition with each other for limited resources (poverty), Romanians are not as performance-driven and need to like what they do and who they work with. In times of great personal uncertainty and stress, Romanians traditionally seek refuge in their Orthodox faith.

---

[12] according to Hofstede's original estimates.

This is what the relation between Romanian and German cultural values looks like in a diagram based on G. Hofstede's dimensions:

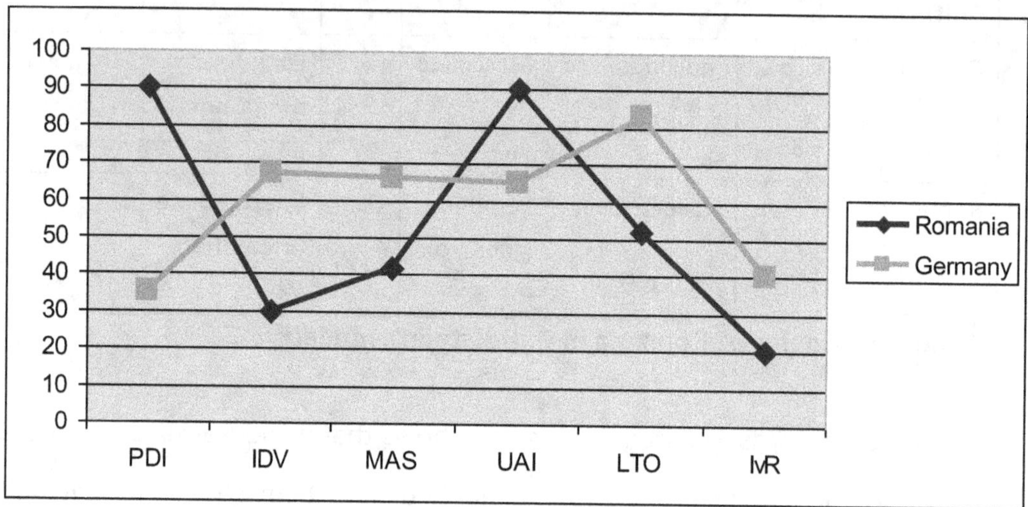

Fig. 1. Germany vs. Romania according to G. Hofstede's cultural dimensions

However, a nation-wide study conducted by Gallup Romania using Hofstede's methodology and his VSM94 values survey questionnaire (for the business consulting company Interact) shortly before 2005 showed very different results:

Parameter / Culture	PDI	IDV	MAS	UAI	LTO
Germany	Low PDI 35	Individualistic 67	Masculine 66	High UA 65	LTO 83
Romania	Low PDI 31	Barely collectivistic 49	Feminine 39	High/mod. UA 61	STO 42

Table 3. Germany vs. Romania in G. Hofstede's model – a different version[13]

---

[13] according to Luca, A., "A Study on the Position of Romania on Hofstede's Cultural Dimensions, Version II", for Interact, Bucharest, 2005 - online:

This time Romanians scored suspiciously low in PDI, and the testers believe that happened because the respondents did not answer openly but rather as they thought it was expected of them or how they believed the ideal working environment *should* be. The Interact team estimates a more realistic PDI for Romania to be around 70 – in line with the concentration of power observable in society and with the attitude of pleasing one's superiors and the acceptance of abusive actions. The low value indeed indicates that Romanians *preferred* (or said they preferred) a more participative, cooperative management style. The researchers concluded that the large gap between desired and actual behavior might testify to the so-called Romanian 'authority complex', which "may be at the root of why Romanians obstinately refuse to obey any rule in practice, while at the same time crying out for all sorts of rules and regulations"[14].

In this survey, Romania ranks only barely collectivistic, and the researchers predicted a steady increase in individualism as financial resources and capitalist business models continued to pour into the country, thus leading to more development.

Probably the best side of 'femininity' is that women are not quite as subordinated, there is much less of a glass ceiling for women in leadership positions in Romania, and crime is usually not very violent, but often limited to petty theft and misdemeanors. It also means that Romanians do not define

---

https://alingavreliuc.files.wordpress.com/2010/10/hofstede-romania-comparativ.pdf, 06.04.2016
[14] Luca, A., "A Study on the Position of Romania on Hofstede's Cultural Dimensions, Version II," for Interact, Bucharest, 2005, p. 8

themselves exclusively through their jobs and professional achievements and may be less competitive than other nations.

Romanians can have difficulties dealing with ambiguous situations and different opinions. Actions are typically geared towards survival and rejecting demands by minorities (sexual and otherwise).

The short-term orientation means there are difficulties in planning for the future and that people tend to refer to past experience for quick solutions. The business cycle is rather unstable and Romanians, though creative, often prefer not to take responsibility for innovation.

According to the Interact study of 2005, the ideal management scenario for Romania would be a German structure (more stability, rigor, fairness, decentralization) with a UK-style manager (more approachable). Romanians expect their leader to be strong and earn their respect (because that is what they have been used to and have come to expect) but immediately criticize and resist that behavior if the leader is perceived as too authoritarian (because, ideally, they desire a low PDI environment).

2.1.3. Fons Trompenaars' and Charles Hampden-Turner's model

Fons Trompenaars is a Dutch organizational theorist, management consultant, and author with a Ph.D. from Wharton, who Financial Times dubbed "the new star of the world's management seminar". He specialized in cross-cultural communication and in 1989 founded a consultancy named *Center for International Business Studies*, in which he partnered with another leading management consultant, Charles Hampden-Turner. Charles Hampden-

Turner is a British management philosopher and creator of the *Dilemma Theory*, who has authored 14 books, including *Maps of the Mind*.

Together, they have offered intercultural consulting services to multinational companies such as BP, IBM, Heineken, Motorola, Philips, General Motors, ABN AMRO, ING, Mars, Johnson & Johnson, etc.

In Trompenaars' and Hampden-Turner's view, culture is like "water to a fish".[15] In other words, they see culture as an all-encompassing system crucial to meaningful interaction: "Social interaction, or meaningful communication, presupposes common ways of processing information among the people interacting. These have consequences for doing business, as well as managing across cultural boundaries.[16] For Trompenaars and Hampden-Turner, the slippery concept of culture has to do with what they call "a shared definition of the situation by a group." A culture is made up of different layers: an implicit core of basic assumptions and beliefs, a middle layer made up of norms, values and attitudes, and an explicit outer layer comprising the visible products and "artifacts" of culture, where we would include behaviors, institutions, etc.

Building on Kluckhohn's and Strodtbeck's five categories of problems[17] all cultures have to deal with (social relations, time orientation, activity orientation, man-nature relationship, and human nature), Trompenaars and Hampden-Turner have attempted to analyze cultures based on how they come up with solutions (and what solutions they prefer) to the following questions:

---

[15] Trompenaars, F., Hampden-Turner C., *Riding the Waves of Culture*, Nicholas Brealey Publishing, London, 1997, p. 20
[16] idem.
[17] Kluckhohn, F., Strodtbeck, F.L., *Variations in Value Orientations*, Greenwood Press, Westport, 1961

- What is more important: rules or relationships?
- Do we function as a group or as individuals?
- Do we display our emotions?
- How separate do we keep our private and working lives?
- Do we have to prove ourselves to receive status, or is it given to us?
- Do we do things one at a time or several things at once?
- Do we control the environment or are we controlled by it?

As a result, the seven categories of cultural differentiation Trompenaars and Hampden-Turner have identified are:

1. **Universalism vs. Particularism**

   o Universalistic cultures place high importance on laws, rules, values, and obligations that apply to all individuals at all times. They try to deal fairly with people, based on rules which are considered above personal relationships or particular situations. They use objective processes to reach decisions and tend to believe in equality. Particularistic cultures, on the other hand, believe that each individual circumstance and each individual relationship dictates the rules they live by. Their response to a situation may change based on what is happening and who exactly is involved. Personal circumstances take precedence over abstract rules.

2. **Individualism vs. Communitarianism**

   o Individualistic cultures attach great value to personal freedom, autonomy, and individual achievement. They believe each person can and should make their own decisions and take care of themselves ('each man for himself'). For communitarian (or collectivistic) cultures, the group and its future are more important than the individual. The group provides help, safety, and a sense of belonging in exchange for its members' loyalty. Individualist cultures can also be distinguished by the frequent use of 'I', as opposed to the frequent use of 'we' for communitarian cultures.

3.   **Neutral vs. Emotional**

   o   Neutral cultures do not display their emotions publicly and they believe in self-restraint. They make great efforts to control their emotions and to use reason instead of feelings for guiding their decisions and actions. Outbursts of emotions can discredit a person in the eyes of others. People do not like to reveal what they are feeling or thinking. Emotional cultures are always looking for ways to express their emotions, even in the workplace. They often behave very spontaneously and welcome the show of emotions.

4. **Specific vs. Diffuse**

   o   Specific cultures like to have a clear separation between the work environment and the private realm. Their professional and personal lives are kept separate. They believe that relationships do not have a lot of impact on work objectives and that people can work together well even if they don't have a good personal relationship. Diffuse cultures allow their personal and professional lives to overlap and believe good relationships are vital to their work endeavors.

5. **Achievement vs. Ascription**

   o Achievement-oriented cultures believe that someone's worth is based on what that person does and achieves; they value performance regardless of origins. Ascription-based cultures tend to value people for who they are; origins, power, title, and position matter a lot and should be used and respected accordingly.

6. **Sequential vs. Synchronous time**

   o Similarly to Hall's model, people in sequential cultures tend to do one thing at a time, value punctuality, stick to the plan, and stay on schedule. They consider time to be fixed, finite and valuable. Synchronous-time cultures are flexible in their approach to time and time commitments. For them, the past, present, and future are interwoven and fluid. They often multitask and are not sticklers to plans.

7. **Internal locus of control vs. External locus of control**

   o Cultures that have an internal direction (or locus of control), believe in their ability to control the environment, their lives, and their goals. People in cultures with external direction see themselves and their lives as controlled by the environment, by outer factors, and try to adapt, i.e. to work with or around them. They focus their attention on others and avoid conflicts. Often they are more fatalistic, as they do not perceive the locus of control as being in their hands.

2.1.3.1. Germany vs. Romania in the Trompenaars-Turner model

To assess their seven dimensions of human behavior, Trompenaars and Hampden-Turner presented respondents in workshops with a series of dilemmas (or situations) for each. Interestingly enough, Romania scores quite close to Germany on the universalism scale. Of the three "dilemmas" presented by the researchers for self-evaluation ("the car and the pedestrian", "the bad restaurant" and "the doctor and the insurance company"[18]), Romanian culture scored 88%, 68%, and 44% respectively on the universalism scale, with Germany scoring 87% and 61% for the first two situations (sadly, it is missing in the third). This generates an average score of 66.6% for Romania and 74% for Germany. The numbers are not that far apart but should be taken with a certain degree of skepticism since they are self-declared and since the dilemmas were offered in workshops, presumably in corporate settings, so their degree of representativeness in the overall population is open to debate.

In terms of individualism[19], when asked to consider their quality of life and whether individual freedoms were preferable, Germans (53% opting for individual freedom) scored considerably lower than Romanians (81%), but it is necessary to keep in mind that the research was conducted in Romania not long after the fall of communism, when liberty and the newly found freedoms

---

[18] Trompenaars, F., Hampden-Turner C., *Riding the Waves of Culture*, Nicholas Brealey Publishing, London, 1997, pp. 33-39
[19] Trompenaars, F., Hampden-Turner C., *Riding the Waves of Culture*, Nicholas Brealey Publishing, London, 1997, pp. 51-57

were extremely desirable. When asked to consider what job was preferable, 62% of respondents in Germany preferred a job where individual *credit* is received, compared with only 57% in Romania. But the percentage of people opting for individual *responsibility* was only 36 in Germany compared to 64 in Romania! An aggregate index would thus result in approximately 50.33% individualism in Germany as opposed to 67.33% in Romania. This is significant because most intercultural models place Germany very high up on the individualism scale, while Romania ranks much lower. In reality, Romanians like to be free, independent, receive credit, and even take responsibility if it allows them to profile themselves, stand out, and gain – whereas the Germans appear in many respects more egalitarian, communitarian, and consensus-seeking (conflict-avoiding society). One of the most typical characteristics readily observed by many Romanians living in Germany, in my discussions with them, has been the German trait of "shunning responsibility." This certainly appears to be confirmed by Trompenaars' research. However, in a subsequent study Germany is shown to have much flatter hierarchical structures compared to the "family culture" of organization in Romania, with its more paternalistic traits.[20] 87% of German respondents said they preferred to be left alone to do their job, as opposed to only 48% of Romanians![21]

Unfortunately, there is no research data on Romania regarding affectivity in Trompenaars' book *Riding the Waves of Culture*, but 35% of the German

---

[20] see also Thomas, A., Rubatos, A., *Beruflich in Rumänien*, Vandenhoeck&Ruprecht, Göttingen, 2011

[21] Trompenaars, F., Hampden-Turner C., *Riding the Waves of Culture*, Nicholas Brealey Publishing, London, 1997, pp. 160-163

respondents declared they would not show their emotions openly at work[22] (i.e. a high level of neutrality). Information gathered through informal interviews with friends and colleagues in Romania, as well as the Latin heritage of Romanians argue in favor of more emotionality in the Romanian workplace, where arguments and emotions are not infrequent. It must be said, though, that there is a certain degree of indirectness in Romania as well, and conflicts usually fester for a long time before they break out into the open. Romanians will not openly show emotions or fight with their superiors, although they might get very angry and openly admonish inferiors.

Again, Trompenaars' book presents no research data for Romania in terms of the culture being specific or diffuse and we have to rely on evidence from other sources (literature, informal observation, interviews, local information on workplace practices, media). Quite a few multinational (and local) companies in Romania offer joint, company-paid vacations for their employees' families, team buildings, company parties, etc. In exchange, their employees are often available by phone after working hours or on vacation, they almost always invite their bosses, work colleagues, and business associates to their weddings, christenings, and other major personal events (sometimes even inviting them to act as godparents).[23] This makes the case for a more diffuse society. On the other hand, the German respondents have an aggregate score of 79% (83% and 75%, respectively, in the two situations presented[24]) in

---

[22] Trompenaars, F., Hampden-Turner C., *Riding the Waves of Culture*, Nicholas Brealey Publishing, London, 1997, p. 70
[23] Lizard, T.W., Gheorghiu O. C., How to survive Romania, Lizard&Partners, Bucharest, 2014
[24] Trompenaars, F., Hampden-Turner C., *Riding the Waves of Culture*, Nicholas Brealey Publishing, London, 1997, pp. 86-93

rejecting company intervention in the private sphere or an expansion of corporate responsibility in the personal sphere (specific, separate). Even in terms of organizational preferences, only 66% of Romanian respondents opted for function as the main criterion of organization (the rest preferring personality as the main pivot, which would also seem to suggest more diffuse work and personal lives), as opposed to 92% of Germans in favor of function.[25]

In terms of achievement vs. ascription, only 20% of Romanian respondents disagreed that the most important thing in life is to behave as it suits you – compared to 40% of Germans.[26] Thus, both cultures are relatively ascriptive, but Germany is more on the 'getting things done' side. When asked to rate whether respect is granted based on family background, 74% of Germans disagreed, and there is no data on Romania. The conclusion we derive is that, overall, Germany is a more achievement-oriented society. (There is strong ascription based on academic titles in Germany, but since an academic title is still a measure of achievement, this remains ambiguous.)

With regard to time management, temporal relationships, and dealing with time in general (which is becoming an increasingly complex issue), Trompenaars' and Hampden-Turner's research yields some interesting results. On a scale of 1 to 7, where 7=years, 6=months, 5=weeks, 4=days, 3=hours, 2=minutes, and 1=seconds, Germany scores fairly in the middle (between 4 and 5) in terms of temporal horizon, making it a present-oriented society.[27] Past,

---

[25] Trompenaars, F., Hampden-Turner C., *Riding the Waves of Culture*, Nicholas Brealey Publishing, London, 1997, pp. 168-169
[26] Trompenaars, F., Hampden-Turner C., *Riding the Waves of Culture*, Nicholas Brealey Publishing, London, 1997, pp. 104-106
[27] Trompenaars, F., Hampden-Turner C., *Riding the Waves of Culture*, Nicholas Brealey Publishing, London, 1997, pp. 126-129

present, and future overlap a little, but not much, indicating that the level of synchronicity is low. The average German time horizon for the past is above 5 (weeks to months), and the average German time horizon for the future is also slightly above 5 (in other words, the Germans' idea of the future is not too close, not too distant – but Germans do tend to plan several weeks to several months ahead). There is no data in Trompenaars' research about Romania, but studies performed with different other models and a look at the Romanian public and political scene, for instance, all suggest that there is a higher degree of synchronism (in E.T. Hall's terminology, a more *polychronic* society), that time is fluid and the future rarely viewed as stable or scheduled rigidly in advance. Plans change and are adjusted 'on the go', in the short term. Multitasking (doing several things at once) and spontaneity are the norm.

Finally, perhaps the most unexpected differences between Germany and Romania can be observed in terms of their relationship to nature. According to Trompenaars' and Hampden-Turner's research, 30% of German respondents believe it is worth trying to control important natural forces, like the weather, as opposed to 68% of Romanians![28] Again, I have to caution against hasty conclusions and draw attention to the fact that this research was done in a country recently freed from dictatorship, in which the technological backwardness was a reason for embarrassment. Severe droughts, floods, and rough winters still cause major disruptions in Romania to this day, with most people merely trying to 'make do' and adjust passively to the elements. In this light, the Romanian percentage points seem quite exalted, more 'wishful

---

[28] Trompenaars, F., Hampden-Turner C., *Riding the Waves of Culture*, Nicholas Brealey Publishing, London, 1997, p. 142-144.

thinking' (normative response) than anything else. German realism and rationality are probably the cause of the much lower German figure. When asked if they believed that what happens to them is their own doing (in other words, if they have agency and control over their fates), a surprising percentage of Romanian responded yes: 69% (compared to 66% of Germans). For a country known for its fatalistic mindset[29], this is quite astonishing. Overall, the aggregate scores for this dimension are 48% inner-orientation for the Germans (which is akin to having more of an external locus of control), and 68.5% inner-orientation for Romania. It would seem that the Romanian participants felt more capable of influencing their environment and destiny than the Germans – a fact that is somewhat contradicted by the realities of political participation[30] and the ubiquitous anecdotal evidence of Romanian fatalism captured by the everyday phrase, "What can you do? This is the way life is..." ("*Ce să-i faci? Asta-i viața...*").

Research by Dr. Daniel David (2015) from the Babes-Bolyai University also places Romanians lower on the self-determination scale (at least compared to the USA) and thus seems to invalidate Trompenaars' findings[31].

Below, you can see a simplified version of Trompenaars' data about Romania and Germany (using the aggregated averages mentioned above, where applicable).

---

[29] See most famous Romanian folk ballad, *Miorița*

[30] Over the past decade, rates of participation in Parliamentary elections have been very low - around 41.72% of registered voters. Even in the hotly contested 2014 Presidential election, only 53.17% of Romanians cast their vote.

[31] David, D., *Psihologia poporului român*, Ed. Polirom, Bucharest, 2015, p. 160, table 3.12.

Parameter/ Culture	Univ./ Partic.	Indiv./ Comm.	Neutr./ Emot.	Spec./ Diff.	Achiev./ Ascription	Seq./ Synchr.	Inner- /Outer- oriented
Germany	74	50.33	35	79	40	4.69	48
Romania	66.66	67.33	no data	no data	20	no data	68.5

Table 4. Germany vs. Romania in Trompenaars' and Hampden-Turner's model (average aggregate scores)

Using our common sense, cultural sources (media, literature), and practitioner experience to make an informed choice and fill in the blanks of the Trompenaars & Hampden-Turner model concerning Romania, the two cultures might look something like this on a chart:

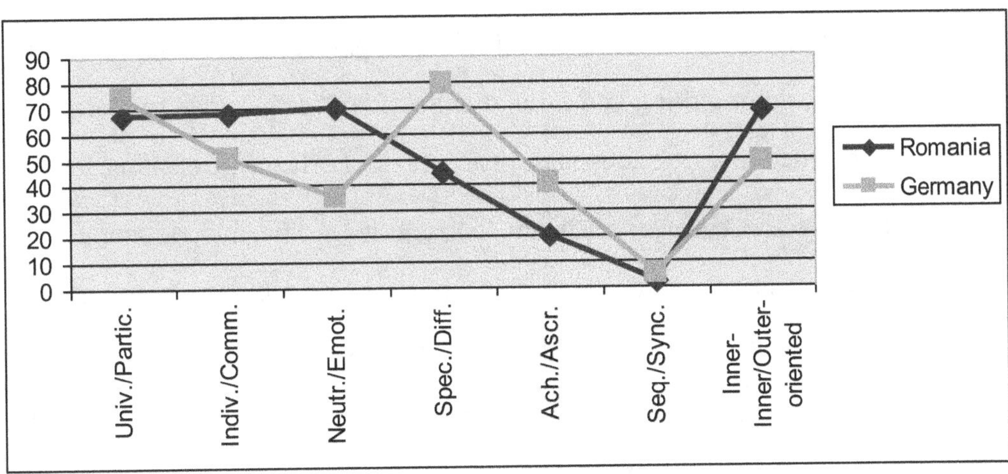

Fig. 2. Germany vs. Romania according to the Trompenaars and Hampden-Turner categories

2.1.4. More models (R. D. Lewis, GLOBE, E. Meyer, etc.)

Richard D. Lewis is one of Britain's foremost linguists. He speaks 10 European and 2 Asiatic languages and was tutor to Empress Michiko of Japan and other members of the Imperial family. He founded Richard Lewis Communications, an international institute of intercultural and language training. Lewis believes that by focusing on the cultural roots of national behavior, we can foresee with a good degree of accuracy how others will react and respond to us in both social and business settings. In his famous book, *When Cultures Collide* (1999, 2004), he lays out his concept of linear-active, multi-active, and reactive cultures. Lewis's work is concerned with the way people perceive time and how they act within that concept of time. In brief, his delineations are as follows:

- **Linear-active** cultures plan, schedule, organize, prefer definite action chains, do one thing at a time, manifest strict adherence to hierarchies and procedures, seriousness, property, and privacy (Germans, Swiss)

- **Multi-active** cultures are lively, loquacious, and flexible, do many things at once, like to joke, to combine business and pleasure, private and public, plan according to subjective importance (Latins, Arabs)

- **Reactive** cultures prioritize courtesy and respect, listening quietly and calmly, reacting carefully, saving face (Japanese, Chinese, Finns)

R.D. Lewis also considers language a major factor in our cultural 'programming', and often a very constraining one when we suddenly find ourselves in different cultures with different perceptions, interpretations, or reactions. He calls language a "strait-jacket phenomenon"[32]. Even when people share a common experience, the way these impressions are organized by the mind has a lot to do with language. The language we speak, according to the Sapir-Whorf hypothesis of linguistic relativity, largely influences our way of thinking, let alone how we express things. He thus shifts the focus of culture acquisition from mere socialization through the behavior and personal example of those around us (parents, teachers, peers, society), to language. It could, however, be argued that the correlation between language structures, lexis, and culture cuts both ways, and that causality is possible in the opposite direction as well (i.e., the way we are and live influences the language that eventually emerges). Culture decides what gets encoded in language.

In her excellent 2014 book, *The Culture* Map, Erin Meyer takes a more functional approach, looking at the pragmatic aspects of conducting business across cultures, such as:

- Communication style (low-context vs high-context)

- Evaluating and giving negative feedback (directly vs. indirectly)

- Persuading (principles-first vs. applications-first)

- Leadership style (egalitarian vs. hierarchical)

- Decision-making (consensual vs. top-down)

- Trusting (task-based vs. relationship-based)

- Disagreeing (confrontational vs. confrontation avoidance)

- Scheduling (linear time vs. flexible time).

---

[32] Lewis, R.D., *When Cultures Collide*, Nicholas Brealy Publishing London, 2004, p.17

In recent years, many language services providers have also sought to expand their knowledge and their services into the realm of intercultural communication. One such example is the language school Berlitz, which founded a company called TM Corp to create and implement what they call the Cultural Navigator[33].

According to this, the ten most important dimensions of culture affecting human behavior are:

- **TIME** (tangible vs., intangible; past vs. present vs. future; fixed vs. fluid; single focus - monochronic vs. multitasking - polychronic; sequential vs. synchronic)

- **ACTION** (doing vs. being)

- **COMMUNICATION** (high-context vs. low-context; direct vs. indirect; expressive vs. instrumental; formal vs. informal; self-confident vs. conciliatory vs. confrontational; neutral vs. emotional)

- **SPACE** (public vs. private)

- **POWER** (hierarchy vs. equality)

- **INDIVIDUALISM** (individualism vs. collectivism; universalistic vs. particularistic)

- **COMPETITIVENESS** (feminine vs. masculine; how are people motivated; incentives — is good work ethic reinforced and encouraged/repaid? cooperative vs. competitive/aggressive; achievement vs. ascription)

---

[33] available from TM Corporation, https://tmcorp.culturalnavigator.com/CN7/default.aspx, 06.06.2016

- (Information) **STRUCTURE** (order vs. flexibility; stability vs. change; clarity vs. ambiguity, specific vs. diffuse)

- **THINKING** (inductive vs. deductive reasoning)

- **ENVIRONMENT** (control vs. harmony vs. submission/constraint; do we control the environment or does it control us?)

Another model of culture is that put forth by the GLOBE Research in the 1990s. Its premise is that the effectiveness of leadership is highly contextual, depending on the underlying norms, values, cultural assumptions, and beliefs of the people being led. Its dimensions are:

- Uncertainty Avoidance

- Power Distance

- Institutional Collectivism

- In-Group Collectivism

- Gender Egalitarianism

- Assertiveness

- Future Orientation

- Performance Orientation

- Humane Orientation (how altruistic, generous, caring a society is).

The GLOBE model assigns cultures in clusters, according to levels of similarity. Germany is part of the Germanic cluster along with Austria, the Netherlands, and German-speaking Switzerland. Romania is most likely located at the intersection between the Latin European (Italy, Spain, Portugal, France) and Eastern European (Greece, Hungary, Poland, Albania, Russia, etc.) clusters.

Certainly, most of these models parallel their predecessors, but their main strength lies in managing to bring together a more complete array of dimensions in a very coherent and orderly structure, which aims to mirror more accurately the society at large.

2.1.4.1. Germany vs. Romania in other models

While Germany is discussed at length in the Lewis model (2004) as an almost textbook case of strong linear-active culture, Romania is not yet present. We can only assume it can be assimilated to other Latin, Greek, and multi-active cultures, as that is what the current on-site evidence overwhelmingly suggests.

In his chapter on Germany, R.D. Lewis notes: "Basic characteristics of German business culture are a mono-chronic attitude towards the use of time, e.g. a desire to complete one action chain before embarking on another; a strong belief that they are honest, straightforward negotiators; and a tendency to be blunt and disagree openly rather than going for politeness or diplomacy"[34]. By contrast, the Italians and the Greeks, probably the closest placeholders for Romanian culture, are described as follows:

- "The Italians (...) are excellent **communicators** and combine ultra-keen perception with ever-present **flexibility**. (...) Italians like to share details of families, holidays, hopes, aspirations, disappointments, preferences. (...) they do not automatically believe that Italian must be best."[35]

---

[34] Lewis, R.D., *When Cultures Collide*, Nicholas Brealy Publishing, London, 2004, p. 199.
[35] Lewis, R.D., *When Cultures Collide*, Nicholas Brealy Publishing, London, 2004, p. 237.

(Especially in private and among co-nationals, Romanians will continuously complain about how bad all things Romanian are. With foreigners, however, they desperately want to be liked. Although they might accept criticism of their country and usually appear docile and compliant, refraining from openly defying a foreigner – or any person of authority for that matter – inside, national sentiment can run pretty high. However, their levels of national pride are average, Romanians are generally not chauvinistic.[36])

- "Greece is a **tactile** culture. Its distance of comfort is similar to the Italian, hugging and kissing are common. (...) The Greek view of leadership is somewhat similar to the French conception – that is, rooted in rational argument and skill in oratory. Mastery of the language is seen as essential for commanding the respect of subordinates".[37] (A quick look at the Romanian press one year after the election of the first President belonging to the German minority will show just how important this is to Romanians, too. President Iohannis is often dubbed "the mute president" for his German style of leadership – slow, laconic, dry, heavy, and reserved.) Concerning the Greeks, R.D. Lewis goes on to add another thing that is also typical of Romanian culture, namely, "The multi-active nature of the Greeks means that they are often late for appointments. (...) Greeks are excellent hosts and

---

36 David, D. ,*The Psychology of Romanians*, Ed. Polirom, Bucharest, 2015, p.162, table 3.12
37 Lewis, R.D., *When Cultures Collide*, Nicholas Brealy Publishing, London, 2004, p. 252.

their **hospitality** can be embarrassing. Flowers or a cake are suitable gifts for hostesses."[38] (The same is true for Romania.)

Parameter/Culture	Behavior type
Germany	**Linear-active** (typical)
Romania	**Multi-active** with *relative reactivity* and indirectness in face of authority

Table 5. Germany vs. Romania in the Lewis model

If you truly want to contrast Germany and Romania, plot the two cultures on Erin Meyer's (2014) map – they will appear at opposite ends of the spectrum. In the TM Corp and GLOBE models, Romania and Germany will most likely end up on opposite sides for almost every dimension as well, with the possible exception of individualism and uncertainty avoidance.

Particularly, the GLOBE evaluation of leadership styles places the Germanic cultures very high on a performance-oriented, participative, and autonomous leadership style, while the Latin European and Eastern European cultures rank much lower on the participative scale, about the same on the autonomous scale, and much higher than the Germanic on the self- or group-protective scale.[39]

---

[38] Lewis, R.D., *When Cultures Collide*, Nicholas Brealy Publishing, London, 2004, p. 253.
[39] Hoppe, M.H., GLOBE, http://www.inspireimagineinnovate.com/pdf/globesummary-by-michael-h-hoppe.pdf, (published 2007), 06.06.2016, p. 4

2.2. Conclusions

Social psychology has shown that the human brain prefers to work with categories (Allport 1954) and that comparison across categories is difficult (comparing apples with oranges, for instance). Intergroup contact can help reduce prejudice. Therefore we will now attempt to map the two cultures side by side, along identical categories of analysis, to facilitate comparison.

This allows us to see more readily where they overlap, whether there are similarities and common ground, and where they almost completely diverge - and how. I consider this to be very helpful for finding and building common ground in cross-cultural communication. If we summarize and synthesize the findings of the previously discussed models to paint a schematic picture of the two cultures, this is what an outline of their specificities might look like along some basic categories of human existence and interaction:

Category	GERMANY	ROMANIA
TIME	**Monochronic:** sequential, one thing at a time, strict planning, linear-active, longer-term orientation.	**Polychronic:** synchronous, spontaneous, multi-tasking, fluid, multi-active; present-oriented (shorter-term, immediate future).
SPACE	**Distance:** privacy, separate spheres, little physical contact, autonomy.	**Closeness:** warmth; open and tactile; overlapping spheres, interdependence.

Category	GERMANY	ROMANIA
COMMUNICATION AND EMOTIONS	**Low-context**: very explicit, clear, detailed, and direct communication.	**High-context**: a lot of information is implicit, non-verbal/indirect, or incomplete, "coded", hinted, difficult for outsiders.
	Neutral and specific: separation of work/private life, no display of emotions in public, strong self-control. Communication is rather formal and instrumental; order; clarity and stability.	**Emotional and diffuse**: highly emotional; too much self-control is seen as dogmatic (lacking in expressivity and personality). Communication is more informal and animated/expressive; communication with superiors is more indirect; flexibility and ambiguity.
STRUCTURE AND ACTION	**Universalistic**: Rules, order, and regulations are very important, enforced rigidly, and observed by all.	**Universalistic (declared) but with a clear tendency towards particularism**: Order is appreciated, but individual needs are more important; ambivalence towards authority; rules seen as flexible and often bent to suit personal/immediate needs.

Category	GERMANY	ROMANIA
	High uncertainty avoidance tactics: rules, regulations, punctuality, process, and procedures.	**High uncertainty avoidance** tactics: family ties, connections, conservatism, suspicion, traditions, work, religion.
	Restraint: systematic saving, frugality, job-sharing.	**Restraint**: pessimism, adjusting one's needs; splurging and fasting.
HUMAN RELATIONSHIPS & COMPETITIVENESS	**Masculine**: goal and performance-oriented, assertive and direct; focus on doing; achievement-oriented; neutral; competitive but hierarchical and steady.	**Feminine**: weaker focus on facts/goals/results, indirect, more focus on people, relationships, and on confrontation avoidance; focus on *being*; less achievement-oriented; affective yet competitive.
	Individualism	**Collectivism/Relative individualism** (depending on model and context)
	Status orientation: solid education and academic titles, competence and ability, experience, car, house.	**Status orientation**: money, brand products, position and social connections, car, house, travels, prestigious education, level of courteousness.

Category	GERMANY	ROMANIA
POWER	**Low PDI:** power inequality and power concentration are low or limited; federalism.	**High PDI**: high power inequality and power concentration; centralism (yet respondents indicate they would prefer lower PDI).
ENVIRON-MENT	**We control and subdue our environment** (internal control).	**We adjust and adapt to our environment** (external influences).

Table 6. Germany vs. Romania - Specific overall traits and characteristics of national culture based on the most common models of intercultural communication

What is interesting to note here is that, even in those areas where the inner circles of principles and beliefs are the same, their outward manifestations differ! One explanation for this might be the underlying collectivism of Romanians. Thus, in German culture uncertainty avoidance, restraint, and status appear to rest more on the autonomous individual – through self-control, personal effort, abiding by the rules of one's own accord (for restraint and uncertainty avoidance), and personal merit/personal accomplishments (for status) – whereas in Romania both uncertainty avoidance and status have to do with belonging to a 'better' group of people (better information, better clothes, better cars, better connections, superior spirituality, etc.). In Romania, expecting the worst and learning to accept any outcome (indifference), suspicion, and collective pessimism have become coping mechanisms for avoiding high uncertainty and existential angst.

In evaluating the two cultures one must also consider the fact that while Germany has remained a prosperous and stable society over the past 70 years (despite the influx of guest workers since the 1950s), Romania has undergone tectonic upheavals (war-time right-wing dictatorship, communism/cult of personality, bloody revolution, transition to capitalism and democracy). There have been enormous societal changes after the anti-communist revolution of 1989. Many of the older, 'typical' Romanian values have faded, giving rise to different worldviews and models of interaction, as well as to different social norms or rather to a general confusion regarding social norms. Clear values and social institutions have yet to solidify.

Traditionally, Romania was a collectivist culture and to this day is still considered by many researchers as one of the only four collectivist cultures in the EU (alongside Portugal, Greece, and Bulgaria).[40] But a deeper study of current attitudes reveals a clear trend towards increasing individualism (see Trompenaars research). Also, despite traditionally being seen as a friendly, hospitable, and peace-loving people, Romanians have come to exhibit lower levels of benevolence and higher levels of conformity than the Germans.[41] These developments most likely have to do with the increased levels of stress, existential uncertainty, and frustration that result from a long and troubled transition to free-market practices, as well as from chronic injustice

---

[40] David, D., *Psihologia poporului român*, Ed. Polirom, Bucharest, 2015, p.

[41] David, D., *Psihologia poporului român*, Ed. Polirom, Bucharest, 2015, p. 104, table 3.2, p. 105, table 3.4

(corruption), poverty, poor infrastructure, poor public services, and cronyism. In this respect, the Germans can definitely 'afford' to be more relaxed.

According to the World Values Survey, the dominant values in post-communist Romania are traditionalism and survivalism.[42] Dr. David's research shows that while Romanian children tend to have happier childhoods than their German counterparts, their levels of frustration and rage consistently rise above those measured in Germany once they reach adulthood (this is especially true for women).[43]

Currently, Romanians show higher levels of workplace competitiveness and status-orientation than their German counterparts[44], yet lower levels of perseverance and discipline (where perseverance means carrying a task all the way through with a high degree of accuracy and quality). This latter trait goes as far back as the traditional Romanian folk ballad *Monastirea Argeşului* (The Argeş Monastery, also known as *Meşterul Manole*) (16th century), where everything that bricklayers build during the day collapses during the night, and only human sacrifice can ultimately 'glue' the construction together. Romanians are often inconsistent in their actions and change plans (and direction) often and quickly. In Daniel David's own words, Romanians "aim high, they want to be at the top, but often do not know how (not enough discipline) and give up easily or fail to reach the desired results. (...) Also, the

---

[42] Inglehart and Welzel, "The WVS Cultural Map of the World", http://www.worldvaluessurvey.org/WVSContents.jsp, Live cultural map 1981-2015, 06.06.2016
[43] David, D., *Psihologia poporului român*, Ed. Polirom, Bucharest, 2015, p. 110
[44] idem, p. 106-107

socio-cultural environment in which [they] evolve does not enable the transformation of competitiveness into efficiency"[45].

It is probably fair to say that while Germans are typically more rigorous and consistent in their attitudes, actions, and work, Romanians are typically more creative and inventive but less disciplined; their solutions are usually short-term-oriented and lack consistency.

Personal distance is much smaller in Romania, where hugging, kissing, and shaking hands are normal when meeting an acquaintance or a relative (even among men), while Germans need a personal space of at least an arm's length. While Germans in business settings favor long, heavy, factual explanations where everything is touched upon in a structured way, Romanians often digress and do not follow a very clear thread. They prefer flexibility and witty, emotional rhetoric.[46] While Germans prefer written communication in business, in Romania nothing important happens without at least a phone call, preferably a meeting in person. Trust in strangers is much lower in Romania than in Germany[47], and the importance of religion is more than three times as big in Romania compared to Germany[48].

Romanians like to think and decide for themselves if rules are worth following. They are more likely to obey rules and regulations if they trust the issuing authority and if they perceive a personal benefit in following those rules

---

[45] David, D., in Adevărul.ro, online edition, "Cum sunt românii? Concluziile surprinzătoare ale celui mai amplu studiu despre psihologia poporului român", http://adevarul.ro/locale/cluj-napoca/cum-romaniii-concluziile-surprinzatoare-celui-mai-amplu-studiu-despre-psihologia-poporului-roman-1_55a6242df5eaafab2c96cf88/index.html, 06.06.2016

[46] Lewis, R.D., *Cross-Cultural Communication: A Visual Approach*, Transcreen Publications, Warnford, 2008, p. 22

[47] David, D., *Psihologia poporului român*, Ed. Polirom, Bucharest, 2015, p.123, fig. 3.12

[48] David D., *Psihologia poporului român*, Ed. Polirom, Bucharest, 2015, p. 115, fig. 3.9.

or a major loss in case of non-compliance. They tend to disregard or bend rules that appear absurd/arbitrary or unfair (for instance, a pedestrian not being supposed to cross the street simply because the traffic light is red even though no cars are coming from either direction). Romanians are also more emotional in their decisions, more impatient, and rarely plan far ahead due to constantly changing circumstances.

The femininity of Romanian culture is also visible in the lower gender pay gap. Romanian women earn on average 9% less than their male counterparts and are quite present in management positions[49] - especially in the large urban centers. The situation is different in the countryside, and it is also the case that the more feminized an industry is, the lower the wages.[50] By contrast, in Germany over the last decade the pay gap between men and women was approximately 22%, and although a series of measures and quotas have since been enforced, it can still rise to almost 30% for certain management positions.[51]

Generally speaking, Romanians do not exhibit a high level of socio-political violence (although this has seen an upward trend during the pandemic, with the rise of conspiracy theories both online and offline, a rejection of Western values, and a shift towards nationalism and conservative values), nor do they

---

49 Bărbulescu, O. in Profit.ro, online edition, "Femeile câştigă cu 9% mai puţin decât bărbaţii şi sunt hărţuite la muncă. Recomandări pentru firme: munca la domiciliu şi day-care pentru copii", http://www.profit.ro/stiri/social/document-femeile-castiga-cu-9-mai-putin-decat-barbatii-si-sunt-hartuite-la-munca-recomandari-pentru-firme-munca-la-domiciliu-si-day-care-pentru-copii-15430957, 06.06.2016

50 See also a 2021 study on gender inequalities on the Romanian labor market, available at: https://library.fes.de/pdf-files/bueros/bukarest/18613.pdf

51 Kramer, B. in Spiegel.de, online edition, "Gehaltsunterschiede der Geschlechter: Warum Frauen weniger verdienen http://www.spiegel.de/unispiegel/jobundberuf/gender-pay-gap-warum-bekommen-frauen-weniger-lohn-a-1024229.html, 06.06.2016

manifest much of a civically or ecologically-justified collectivism, but rather a type of collectivism centered on family, work, and religion. A 2018 referendum organized by conservative forces to outlaw same-sex marriage failed for lack of sufficient voter turnout, but of the 21% of registered voters that did show up at the polling stations, a whopping 93% voted against same-sex marriage.

In their lax adherence to rules in Romania yet general compliance while abroad, Romanians exhibit both individualism and gregariousness (do what everybody else does). Recent research by Shulruf and colleagues (2011) has demonstrated that Romanian students are indeed more individualistic than initially suggested by Hofstede's model[52]. High school students are also increasingly involved in fighting corruption in their schools and exposing it publicly via social media. It is, therefore, likely that the new generations will move Romania closer to Western-type individualism.

---

[52] David, D., *Psihologia poporului român*, Ed. Polirom, Bucharest, 2015, p. 180

3. Check Out Those Standards! Germany and Romania According to Self-image and Hetero-Comparison

Cultural standards – although essentially statistical generalizations – represent the foundation of an orientation system devised to help analyze, evaluate, and carry out interactions. A cultural standard includes those accepted, typical, and/or 'obligatory' norms and behaviors shared by a group of people or a culture. They are often subconscious, often become starkly apparent in interactions among different cultures, can help steer and influence these interactions, but they do not represent a final description of a culture in its entirety. They are merely useful abstract instruments.

3.1. The German cultural profile: Cultural orientations, values, and narratives of German culture

According to a group of researchers around Alexander Thomas from the University of Regensburg (Germany) and thanks to the work of Sylvia Schroll-Machl (2003), the German cultural profile can be said to consist of the following typical traits (or "standards")[53]:

❖ *Task orientation, rule orientation, structure orientation*:
  o Germans prefer to stick to a structured and tested way of doing things (a process).

---

[53] Thomas, A., Schroll-Machl, S., Kammhuber, S., *Handbuch Interkulturelle Kommunikation und Kooperation – Band 2. Länder, Kulturen und interkulturelle Berufstätigkeit*, Vandenhoeck & Ruprecht, Göttingen, 2003, pp. 74-82.

- o Germans have an inner need for order and clear orientation, rules are important, justified, and necessary because they reduce uncertainty and enable constant results.
- o Germans love structures. Rules (both implicit and explicit) are present everywhere in human interactions, can be quite rigid, and sometimes more important than people.
- o Germans have a strong need for clear orientation and adhere to structures because they like to control their environment and avoid uncertainty.
- o Property and money are considered very important and taken very seriously. Germans are very orderly, they like to control life. (Which is also why many of them are wary of 'better'/different ways of doing things.)
- o Fixed procedure takes precedence over spontaneous creativity.

❖ ***Strict time planning, clear and detailed timetables, conscientiousness:***
- o Intensive planning is seen as the best solution to avoid mistakes, and assigned tasks are taken very seriously.
- o To foreigners, Germans appear obsessed with timetables and with planning everything months in advance. (They also think a lot about retirement and are constantly concerned with saving money).
- o Time is considered a limited and very precious good, which has to be used most effectively. Punctuality is key. Germans are both present and long-term-oriented.

- o Germans also prefer to do things sequentially, one after the other, and focus on one thing at a time.
- o They do not change their carefully laid out plans easily, and often remain inflexible when external circumstances change, considering them 'details of secondary importance'.
- o Schedules and instructions are binding.
- o There is an expectation among Germans of high self-discipline and individual responsibility. They are thorough.
- o They are earnest, serious, and consistent, and believe that certain ideas, principles, and tasks are too important to be taken lightly.

❖ *Self-control, factual thinking, objective, and autonomous criteria:*
- o Germans identify very strongly with their profession or occupation. They take their roles seriously.
- o Showing emotions in public or deciding based on emotions is disavowed. When considering issues, they look for calm, rational arguments.
- o Germans believe that they have to do the right thing not the popular one and that they generally do better quality work than others.
- o Communication is direct, concrete, factual *("sachlich")*, and sometimes cutting.
- o Authenticity, honesty, objective fairness is seen as more important than harmony, while perfectionism is a driving force.
- o Self-worth is defined according to abilities, level of performance, and achievements (materialism and efficiency).

o   Generally, Germans are strict and disciplined.

❖ *Distance and discretion:*

o   Germans are usually very reserved during first contact and they do not actively seek to make contact or become acquainted with people they do not know. This is called the principle of non-interference. They need a bigger personal space bubble.

o   Colleagues that get along well at work do not automatically become friends in real life, as these two spheres are very separate. The boss has authority only in the workplace.

o   Germans make a clear distinction between the person and the role and try to keep emotions and rationality separate.

o   It usually takes very long to truly get to know a German, as they tend to be very private, but once you do, they open up and are usually loyal friends for the long haul. This process goes from neutral, conformist behavior according to the person's *role*, to *gradually* getting closer and opening up emotionally step-by-step, to friendliness and warmth, and finally to full access to the other's *core* and to mutual commitment.

o   For Germans, expressing emotions is not typical, they are taught to be more introverted and repressed. They are not a tactile culture.

❖ *Low-context communication and directness:*

- o Germans communicate directly and explicitly what they want and expect, what they consider to be good or bad, even at the cost of appearing tactless to other cultures.
- o Their *yes* is *yes* and their *no* is *no*, prices are seen as objective and fair, so they are not in the habit of negotiating.
- o Germans rely very little on context and describe everything clearly and in detail so that it is clear even for those who are unfamiliar with the context.
- o The *what* is more important than the *how*.
- o Germans speak mostly about things, plans, objective issues, the factual content is the most important in communication. They prefer not to leave margin for interpretation – which is why they prefer written communication. Almost everything is taken literally, and little to no importance is placed on the relationship side of the communication.
- o They can appear confrontational (or 'rude') to other cultures, although they generally prefer consensus (*"Wir müssen jetzt nicht diskutieren!"*).
- o The Germans are straightforward.

❖ *Separation of life areas:*

- o Co-workers are not necessarily seen as friends or confided in – personal issues remain personal.
- o The more objectively one communicates and acts at work, the more professional they are considered by the Germans.

- o The Germans separate their public or work life from their private or family one.
- o Roles, competencies, and an effective functioning within the organization are more important than personal liking.
- o Work and family rarely mix and most Germans expect their employers to respect their private life once they have left the company at the end of the day.

❖ *Individualism*:

- o Germans are individualistic and autonomous.
- o Society is atomized, the nuclear family is the rule, with extended family participating only at important events.
- o Old people are often lonely and live apart from their children.
- o They are also individualistic in the workplace and expect respect for individual needs and convictions.

❖ *Status orientation:*

- o Status has to do with academic achievement, competence, experience, ability.
- o Academic titles, especially Ph.D. degrees are very important and confer high status. They are mentioned on all business cards, correspondence as well as in written and spoken communication.
- o People with Ph.D. degrees should always be addressed as *Doktor*. But even other certified professions expect this kind of respect. A

Fremdsprachenkorrespondentin (foreign language assistant) might feel offended if called a secretary.

- o According to a 2014 FORSA survey, 38% of Germans view their house, and 35% their car as a status symbol.[54] 67% of their "dream cars" are German cars, so owning a good German car is perceived as a symbol of success.

These traits coincide with or are similar to previously presented work by foreign researchers (see previous chapters). I would like to add **environmentalism** to the list.

Germans traditionally have great respect for nature and trees – decorating the Christmas tree is a tradition that originated in the German environment (in spring, the Germans will even decorate their bushes with Easter eggs). The Germans are linked to the early Germanic tribes of the North German Plain and southern Scandinavia, and Germanic and Celtic paganism appear to have involved sacred oak groves and the veneration of the Yule Tree. Over the past 15 years, the Green parties have constantly received upward of 8% of the votes cast for Parliament (Bundestag)[55], and they are currently (2016) the leading political force in Baden-Württenberg, a state where a huge infrastructure project (Stuttgart 21), meant to upgrade the railway, was delayed and almost stopped by ecological protesters due to the cost and environmental concerns. It was a combination of the same (cost and environmental damage) that

---

[54] Cosmosdirekt press release, https://www.cosmosdirekt.de/veroeffentlichungen/autostudie-auftakt-48836/, 06.06.2016
[55] Bundestag.de, http://www.bundestag.de/bundestag/wahlen/ergebnisse_seit1949/244692, 06.06.2016

prompted the populations of Munich (in 2013) and Hamburg (in 2015) to reject a bid by their cities to host the Winter Olympics of 2022, and the Summer Olympics of 2024 respectively.

Environmentalism sometimes takes on near-religious connotations (blind faith in bio-certifications, an obsession with lower emissions, low electromagnetic radiation, gluing oneself to the tarmac to prevent traffic, etc.), while in reality the data shows that Germans produce huge amounts of trash and waste[56], own ever more electronic equipment, and drive ever bigger and heavier cars[57] which do not always comply with emissions regulations (see recent Volkswagen and Audi scandals). A recent study by BAuA (Bundesanstalt für Arbeitsschutz und Arbeitsmedizin) even claims that the majority of so-called 'dangerous' products used in Germany are now German-made.[58] According to EUROSTAT, in 2016 the Romanians were producing the least trash per capita in the EU (poverty means less packaging, more re-use, less consumption or consumption directly from the household, small subsistence farming, etc.). However, Germans recycle much more than the Romanians.

Lately, there have been some interesting dynamics in German work culture as well. A 2014 survey by the Manpower Group (an employment agency) shows that 77% of German employees are motivated by good relationships with their

---

[56] Spiegel Online, "WWF Studie: Deutsche werfen 313 Kilo Lebensmittel weg - pro Sekunde", http://www.spiegel.de/wissenschaft/natur/wwf-studie-millionen-tonnen-lebensmittel-landen-im-muell-a-1039485.html, 28.04.2016

[57] Kretzmann, J. in Autobild, online edition, "Zeit zum Abspecken", http://www.autobild.de/artikel/fahrzeuggewicht-frueher-und-heute-1268731.html, 28.04.2016

[58] Dönisch, A. in Business Insider Deutschland, online edition, "Aus Deutschland kommen mehr gefährliche Produkte als aus China — und hier sind einige davon", http://www.businessinsider.de/gefaehrliche-produkte-aus-deutschland-2016-4?utm_source=yahoode&utm_medium=referral&ref=yfp, 18.04.2016

work colleagues, with 45% of them declaring they are happy to maintain nice contact with their work colleagues even after working hours. 67% of the German respondents now prefer flexible working hours, 38% are more motivated when their company offers sports and health-related activities, and 24% like receiving small surprise gifts from co-workers and/or employers![59]

In his 2008 book *Cross-Cultural Communication: A Visual Approach,* R. D. Lewis notes the following about the Germans: "Germans belong to a **data-oriented**, low-context culture, and like receiving **detailed information and instruction** (...). The almost invariable use of the **formal** 'Sie' form in business fits in well with the expectation of **obedience."[60]** As for the German leadership style, it is Lewis' opinion that it consists of putting "the most experienced, best-educated person at the top and he/she instructs and guides meticulously his/her immediate subordinate. Orders are passed down (...) in this manner. Though leadership is consequently **hierarchical and autocratic**, German leaders do listen to suggestions "from the factory floor" (...). In this way, **consensus** plays a part in German business."[61]

Schroll-Machl (2003) gives us a fascinating insight into the historical narrative behind these cultural traits. She suggests that, historically speaking, the enduring isolation of small German states throughout the Middle Ages and later, the ensuing absolutism and the teachings of Protestantism, as well as the

---

[59] Manpower Group Deutschland, "MPG_Infografik_Jobmotivation.pdf, Top 10 Faktoren der Jobmotivation", 2014

[60] Lewis, R.D., *Cross-Cultural Communication: A Visual Approach*, Transcreen Publications, Warnford, 2008, p. 198

[61] Lewis, R.D., *Cross-Cultural Communication: A Visual Approach*, Transcreen Publications, Warnford, 2008, p. 140

repeated destruction most generations of Germans witnessed are essential in understanding the Germans' current psychological and cultural profile.

According to Schroll-Machl, out of the isolation, smallness, and fragmentation that was typical of most German principalities for centuries, a tight inner sense of social integrity emerged, while there existed virtually no contact with the outside world (and it was not considered necessary).[62] This led to distance and the separation of life areas, as well as to a very strict sense of belonging (to this day, in many areas, only those who speak perfect German, look German, and have lived in Germany for generations are considered truly German – so-called „Bio-Deutsche"). In small states, the personal preferences of the ruling class were law and binding for everyone, and the means to identify and punish opponents were always at hand, which led to conformism and self-control. What's more, due to isolation, the rules imposed could not be relativized or put into perspective by contact with other cultures and other ways of doing things. (A common German identity became popular only in the aftermath of the French Revolution, due to the ideas of J. G. Herder.) Fulfilling one's duties became crucial under absolutism and led to more internalized control. Increasing absolutism caused a flight towards the private areas of life, the only ones that were considered outside these tight controls, thus fueling an additional separation between the public and private spheres, between work and home. Small, often crowded territories and the ability to live a good life under such conditions led to a preoccupation with detail and crafts, as well as to a love of structured interaction. Because of small, isolated territories,

---

[62] Thomas, A., Schroll-Machl, S., Kammhuber, S., *Handbuch Interkulturelle Kommunikation und Kooperation – Band 2. Länder, Kulturen und interkulturelle Berufstätigkeit*, Vandenhoeck & Ruprecht, Göttingen, 2003, pp. 84-87

communication had to be explicit to generate no confusion when crossing borders. Time was also strictly regulated.

A slew of consequences can be attributed to Protestantism, too. In this religion, the cultic, mystical aspects are austere and limited, while the intellectual level is exacerbated. It focuses on rationality and frugality, on solving concrete problems without necessarily searching for the absolute. Work and profession became very important. Protestantism cultivates personal responsibility and thus a more linear usage of time, as well as a clear 'either-or' mentality. Additionally, Lutheranism differentiates very clearly between the 'worldly' (the outer layers, with their demands and roles) and the inner faith. If, as Luther preached, the structures of this world are given by God, Christians must submit and conform while still keeping their faith and conscientiously adhering to the commandments of the New Testament; thus, a lot of internal control is necessary to meet all of those demands simultaneously.

Both before and after 1648, personal security and property were chronically at risk for the Germans. This need for security generated a widespread willingness to obey the prince and his rules or structures. Plague epidemics, as well as the experience of destructive wars in every century, combined with an attachment to home and loved ones placed increased importance on efficiency, on the accumulation of property and resources, and on meticulous planning, in the hope of avoiding or at least minimizing those expected negative occurrences. In the 19th century, Germany experienced undoubted progress due to bureaucratization and militarization, thus re-enforcing the value of rigid order and discipline. After 1945, finding the strength to continue as a nation after the atrocities of the extermination camps and the guilt attached to the past required sobriety and modesty in public, a lack of pathos, and a renewed focus on discipline, structured work, and survival. Emotions sparked only in private. To offset their Nazi shame, the Germans started on a steady path of pacifism, humanism, and a social market economy.

Without falling into the trap of environmental determinism, it is my personal opinion that geography, climate, and weather patterns might also have influenced German values and attitudes. Long, dark, and cold winters north of the Alps, as well as cool, short, and often wet summers, not only do not encourage exuberance and laxity but require steady, effective work, as well as careful provisioning in advance. Thick low clouds, enduring rain, and the rather limited number of sunny days, as well as the need to work hard and provide for these conditions probably lead to Germans spending a lot of time indoors with their serious and meticulous crafts, and separate from other people. They do not congregate as often in public nor is life lived mostly outside, in the public eye, as in southern or Mediterranean countries. In Romania, spring typically comes earlier, and summers are long, hot, and dry. The weather is mild, often way into October. The summer vacation is three months long (June-September). Romanians don't typically do much outside when it rains, they simply wait for the rain to go away.

Germans love to be able to walk in nature, and, out of necessity, have grown accustomed to doing that even when the weather is less than pleasant. The institution of the *Matschhose und Gummistiefel* (the wet-weather pants and the rubber boots) may seem odd to visitors from southern countries but is need-based. Very effective and linear use of time is also necessary if one is to fully enjoy the few sunny days as well.

German education also encourages individualism, assertiveness, and orderliness but also (to a certain degree) egalitarianism. Children are allowed to choose what they prefer to do or play, but no child leaves a German *Kindergarten* without tidying up his/her toy corner. Children are not forced to comply but rather allowed to discover teamwork on their own and participate of their own accord. Group projects in school also encourage children to discover and enjoy the benefits of cooperating with their peers, as well as the responsibility of pulling one's weight in a group. As opposed to the Romanian school system, in Germany there is little to no open competition among classmates for grades (children strive to get good grades for access to a theoretical high school or, later, to college, but they are basically up against themselves); the high achievers are not celebrated publicly at the end of the school year and the entire grading process is more neutral, private, and standardized.

3.2. The Romanian cultural profile: Cultural orientations, values, and narratives of Romanian culture

In his 1910 book, *Sufletul neamului nostru - Calități bune și defecte* (The Spirit of Our People - Good Qualities and Flaws), Romanian social scientist and Academy member Constantin Rădulescu-Motru describes the Romanian cultural and psychological profile as a very diverse mosaic of positive and negative traits – which he calls "the soul that is in us and yet lives independently outside of us".[63]   He bases his allegations on his own experience, the experiences of others, proverbs and folk sayings, theoretical knowledge, and rigorous scientific observation. According to him, patriotism should not get in the way of serious research.

The first trait he identifies is **collectivism**, in the form of excessive concern with what other people think, do and say (*"do as the world does"*) – typical, in his view, for young rural nations as Romania was at the time. He notices a lack of clear and thoroughly considered individual opinion[64] and notes that neither the school system nor the church has encouraged such autonomous critical thinking. In his 1937 book *Psihologia poporului român,* (The Psychology of the Romanian People), Rădulescu-Motru details even further the cleft between the Romanians' **apparent individualism** (which he sees as a kind of subjective, anarchical egocentrism: "The Romanian (...) wants to be left to his own devices. The absolute master of his own house. With a piece of property, regardless of how small, but his"[65]) and their underlying collectivism which often renders even a westernized school curriculum ineffective. Romanian peasants continue to do things as they have always done them, not risking their peace of mind or their wealth to get rich in a new industrial endeavor. (In fact, it was Radulescu-Motru's conviction that despite an apparent pattern of individualism, Romanians lacked "initiative in economic and social life, the two characteristics traits of individualism as experienced by the cultured Western peoples and

---

[63] Rădulescu-Motru, C., *Sufletul neamului nostru - Calităţi bune şi defecte*, Ed. A. Baer, Bucharest, 1910, p. 4
[64] Rădulescu-Motru, C., *Sufletul neamului nostru - Calităţi bune şi defecte*, Ed. A. Baer, Bucharest, 1910, p. 6
[65] Rădulescu-Motru, C., *Psihologia poporului român*, Ed. Paideia, Bucharest, 1999, p. 16

constituting bourgeois spirit).[66] This risk aversion (also supported by traditional Romanian proverbs) is consistent with Hofstede's analysis of Romania as a high uncertainty avoidance culture and is probably historically conditioned.

According to Rădulescu-Motru (1910), "when a Romanian is in doubt, it is not because he has a personal opinion to protect, but rather because he does not yet know which party to fall in line with". This leads to terrible uncertainty and inner conflict, which Romanians attempt to alleviate by having the best connections and the best access to the latest news or gossip. Religiosity and nationalism are also traits that are most visible in groups. Personal initiative, personal responsibility, and individual determination to contribute are seen as very weak by Rădulescu-Motru; everybody waits for the other person to become proactive, and only then will they join the cause or an already existing group. Superficial and obsessed with politics, the "typical" Romanian does not dwell too long on his actions or conscience, rather expecting all good things to come from above, from a change in law or politics.

A second trait is a **legendary courage when in a group**, followed closely by **cowardice/apathy when isolated and alone**. In groups, there is a contagion of courage and not of fear. Yet in times of peace and plenty the Romanians prefer to avoid military service or discipline. Also, controlling and using the forces of nature to their benefit is something only done 'when push comes to shove', i.e. in the worst case of utter necessity.

Although collectivistic by nature, the Romanians are not consciously solidary for civic purposes, avoid personal sacrifice and limit themselves to acting in a gregarious manner. Constant imitation and flip-flopping are a result

---

[66] Rădulescu-Motru, C., *Psihologia poporului român*, Ed. Paideia, Bucharest, 1999, p. 16

of this **gregariousness**. Although negative for the needs of a modern state in a modern, competitive world, and rather useless for a future of intense economic competition, this gregariousness was seen by Rădulescu-Motru as the most appropriate weapon for survival throughout the centuries in the troubled geopolitical environment where the Romanian principalities were situated; it was his view that the simple people (the common folk) had relied for a long time on collectivism to 'move as one', which had ensured the bare survival of their villages through the difficult centuries. This had kept the small rural communities together, ensured harmony, maintained language, traditions, and a feeling of national belonging.

In his 1937 book, Rădulescu-Motru also mentions improvisations and **a lack of perseverance** as being typical of Romanians but makes the very important distinction that this is true only when the Romanian works for others instead of for himself.[67] Traditionally, Romanians were very perseverant in working the land and hanging on to it. (This has changed in the 21st century.) This lack of perseverance can be attributed to changed social and political circumstances, to the temptation of easy work as a public servant, for which there was initially very little competition and not enough rigorous training (a lax selection process). He also views a **lack of discipline**, a **disorderly attitude to work** (in spurts, as opposed to the Western "clockwork") as well as **the lack of a commercial spirit** as flaws in the Romanian character: "The Romanian peasant sells almost for nothing the produce which he has in large quantities, but pays a disproportionately large price for goods he needs".[68] One can hardly

---

[67] Rădulescu-Motru, C., *Psihologia poporului român*, Ed. Paideia, Bucharest, 1999, p. 18
[68] Rădulescu-Motru, C., *Psihologia poporului român*, Ed. Paideia, Bucharest, 1999, p. 25

avoid a parallel with Romania's current economic situation, characterized by high commercial deficits (EUR 3.3bln in the first semester of 2015, up by 15% on the previous year, still fairly stable around the same figure in 2022), due to cheap exports of natural resources, coupled with expensive imports of complex, high value-added products.[69]

On the positive side, Rădulescu-Motru mentions "**welcoming, tolerant, justice-loving, religious**" as Romanian qualities.[70]

One must keep in mind, though, that these Romanian attributes, however valid, were those identified almost a century ago. Time and subsequent historical, political, technological, and demographic developments must have influenced the cultural and social fabric of the Romanian people, accentuating some traits and eclipsing others. So, how much has changed? And what are the Romanians like today?

Making use of the rigorous quantitative and qualitative techniques of modern-day social research and a solid body of critical instruments, Daniel David in his 2015 book *Psihologia poporului român - Profilul psihologic al românilor într-o monografie cognitiv-experimentală* (The Psychology of the Romanian People - The Psychological Profile of Romanians in a Cognitive-Experimental Monograph), gives us an updated insight into the mental programming of Romanians in the 21st century.

In terms of **intelligence**, his data shows the Romanians can rise to the challenge and exhibit an intellectual potential equal to those of other European

---

[69] Ghinea, R. in Mediafax, "Deficitul balanţei comerciale a urcat cu 15% în S1",online edition, http://www.mediafax.ro/economic/deficitul-balantei-comerciale-a-urcat-cu-15-in-s1-importuri-30-miliarde-euro-exporturi-27-miliarde-euro-14670007, 28.04.2016

[70] Rădulescu-Motru, C., *Psihologia poporului român*, Ed. Paideia, Bucharest, 1999, p. 25

countries in both children and adults. Unfortunately, the cultural environment does not facilitate the optimal (or maximal) use of this potential, which in turn leads to lower than ideal levels of fluid and crystallized intelligence.[71]

The **creativity** levels of Romanians are also as high as those of the Americans, both in children and in adults. A great number of Romanians (born and raised in Romania) who were later placed in a more stimulating cultural environment (via emigration) have risen to great esteem in their professions, becoming distinguished and internationally acclaimed figures in their respective fields: Gheorghe Emil Palade (SUA) won the Nobel prize for physiology/medicine in 1974, Stefan Hell (Germany) won the Nobel prize for chemistry in 2014, Herta Müller (Germany) won the Nobel prize for literature in 2009, and Elie Wiesel (Israel) won the Nobel Peace Prize in 1986. Mircea Eliade (SUA), Emil Cioran, Constantin Brâncuși, George Enescu and Eugen Ionesco (France) were all leading intellectuals. The abyss between merit and success described by Alina Mungiu-Pippidi (2012) in her analysis, for example, shows that Romania is indeed a less accomplishment-based society, and that merit is rather ascribed than achieved.

Romanian **learning styles** (declared, preferred) are very similar to those in the United States of America. Thus, approximately 65% of Romanians prefer an **extroverted** learning style, over 55% prefer an organized learning style (as opposed to a flexible one), 54% prefer a rational style (over an emotional one) and over 64% prefer a **more practical** rather than theoretical learning style.[72]

---

[71] David, D., *Psihologia poporului român*, Ed. Polirom, Bucharest, 2015, p. 195
[72] David, D., *Psihologia poporului român*, Ed. Polirom, Bucharest, 2015, p. 203

These results could be meaningful not only for education reform but also for foreign executives managing Romanian staff as well.

In terms of **emotional intelligence**, Romanian respondents rank lower than U.S. Americans. This is in line with research showing that in highly individualistic cultures (USA), emotional intelligence as a skill is higher than in collectivistic ones.[73]

In terms of **character and temperament**, Romanians are **flexible** and **emotional** (often volatile), **warm** in interpersonal relationships, **gregarious,** and low in autonomy; they accept authority and traditions more easily and perceive change as difficult; they are **ambitious** and **superstitious, creative,** and **undisciplined.**[74] Romanians also score high in terms of risky and aggressive driving.

Romanians suffer from **low self-esteem** (rank 47 of 53 cultures investigated), but they often compensate.[75] The levels of perceived well-being and happiness are also average (5.7 out of 10, rank 49 out of 169 countries investigated in a World Values Survey between 2010-2014).[76] Life satisfaction in Romania is linked with living standards, good health, economic situation, education, trust, countryside, and lower unemployment.

The life satisfaction of Romanians is increased by participating and socializing in their **faith.**[77] 62.8% of Romanians consider this important. The vast majority of Romanians (85.3% according to the last census of 2022) are

---

[73] David, D., *Psihologia poporului român*, Ed. Polirom, Bucharest, 2015, p. 208
[74] David, D., *Psihologia poporului român*, Ed. Polirom, Bucharest, 2015, p. 212, table 4.4
[75] David, D., *Psihologia poporului român*, Ed. Polirom, Bucharest, 2015, p. 223
[76] David, D., *Psihologia poporului român*, Ed. Polirom, Bucharest, 2015, p.227
[77] David, D., *Psihologia poporului român*, Ed. Polirom, Bucharest, 2015, pp. 227-228

Orthodox[78], and the national church narrative is that the early inhabitants of present-day Romania were converted, in Dobruja, by the Apostle Andrew himself. The combination of Latinity and Orthodoxy represents a huge part of the Romanian identity and is seen as something very unique ('an island of Latinity in a Slavic sea', etc.). Insecurities (such as the Covid-19 pandemic) led, in some cases, to a rather dogmatic embrace of **religious faith** and conservative values, with the simultaneous rejection of science or rational solutions. There is in certain circles, a considerable preference for magical and conspiratorial thinking[79] and a vulnerability to fake news, in which many confused people still take refuge in an attempt to make sense of events. In 2020-2022, Romania saw increased polarization on this issue and others.

In terms of **work and work ethic**, many Romanians consider a decrease in the importance of work to be a bad thing. Their work behavior is generally a **type A work style** (competitive, even aggressive in order to succeed, impatient, multi-tasking under time pressure, a feeling of urgency, verbal and psychomotor activism, easily provoked hostility). Romanians score higher than U.S. Americans in terms of both involvement in their work and dissatisfaction with work, a position best explained by the less developed Romanian economy, where holding a job is crucial, even if the work is not as good or interesting. Romanians are competitive and dedicated in their job, but part of these

---

[78] Source: Cornea O. in Europa Liberă România, https://romania.europalibera.org/a/religie-recensamant2022-romani-/32210549.html, 01.02.2023

[79] The low anti-Covid vaccination rates (under 50% at the end of 2021) show that the anti-vaxxer narrative managed to conquer a lot of minds and hearts in Romania. This has many causes, one of which was inconsistent communication by the authorities, a general distrust of government, but it also has to do with low levels of scientific education and media competence among the general Romanian population.

positive attitudes are offset by their willingness to accept delays and the interference of external factors.

The typical **management style** of Romanians is **transactional** and focuses more on monitoring, avoiding, and punishing errors. (It is interesting to note, in this context, the Interact study (2005) which, starting from Hofstede's research regarding Romania, points out that most Romanians declare they would prefer a German-style organization but a British-style manager.) R.D. Lewis (2008) notes, "in the post-Ceausescu period, modern leadership styles are hampered in their development (...). Business leaders are also affected by the continuing influence of the political apparatus. Romanian managers will gradually develop a style of their own – most likely it will resemble that of Italian managers: autocratic but paternalistic and using emotion as a manipulative tool"[80].

Another very interesting and useful aspect related to work ethic is the **Romanians' motivation for performance (*Achievement Motivation Inventory/AMI*).** Compared to the Germans, the Romanians are **less perseverant but more dedicated**; they also exhibit higher internality (accept that it is up to them), a stronger desire to learn, a higher status orientation, as well as higher dominance, optimism, and competition. Surprisingly, in this research, Romanians score lower than Germans in terms of flexibility of tasks, discipline, daring/courage, and independence (i.e., are less motivated by these factors). Romanian workers are more extroverted.[81]

---

[80] Lewis, R.D., *Cross-Cultural Communication: A Visual Approach*, Transcreen Publications, Warnford, 2008, p. 156

[81] David, D., *Psihologia poporului român*, Ed. Polirom, Bucharest, 2015, p. 245, table 4.7

Where **children** are concerned (and how children are socialized), Wege and his partners (2014) show that Romanian stories and fairy-tales contain **more positive** than negative **emotions**.[82] Intense negative emotions are less present. A British research paper by The Children's Society (2015) ranked Romanian children among the happiest in the world (second only to Colombia), and considerably happier than German kids.[83] A South Korean survey (2015) also ranked Romanian children second most happy in school after the Irish. Romanian children appear to have lower levels of anxiety in elementary and secondary school than their U.S. counterparts (but keep in mind that mobbing and bullying have increased dramatically in Romanian schools over the past couple of years). Anxiety grows with age and especially for women.[84]

Old people have a **positive image** in Romanian society but lifestyle, poverty, and bad diets are risk factors leading to obesity and diabetes.[85]

Romanians believe that all religions are moral, and are more **tolerant** towards other nationalities (ethnic minorities) and religions, but this is usually a **passive** rather than constructive tolerance. They are usually disengaged in terms of world peace, global issues, or foreign policy, and have a moderate attitude to peace. They are willing to fight for their own country but generally do not believe that war is a good way to serve justice.

Daniel David (2015) lists intelligence, creativity, ambition, and competitiveness as the Romanians' strongest virtues, while low discipline,

---

[82] David, D., *Psihologia poporului român*, Ed. Polirom, Bucharest, 2015, p. 259, apud Wege et al (2014)
[83] The Children's Society, "The Good Childhood Report 2015", p. 16, fig. 12
[84] David, D., *Psihologia poporului român*, Ed. Polirom, Bucharest, 2015, pp. 259-263
[85] David, D., *Psihologia poporului român*, Ed. Polirom, Bucharest, 2015, p. 266

distrust, lack of cooperation, and low perseverance, coupled with a tendency towards volatile and exaggerated emotional perceptions are aspects that need to be improved in order to allow those virtues to fully manifest themselves.

To summarize, according to Daniel David (2015), Romanians typically exhibit the following psychological profile:

COGNITION	<ul><li>intellectual potentials comparable with those of modern western cultures,</li><li>an ability to make a good first impression,</li><li>*However*, these potentials cannot always realize themselves and are often offset by an un-stimulating environment and a tendency to exaggerate emotionally.</li></ul>

BEHAVIOR	<ul><li>high levels of competitiveness (ambition), generated by the chronic frustration that they do not get what they deserve and by a desire to prove themselves,</li><li>high commitment to school, although mostly formal (the race to get good grades and titles as status labels)</li><li>high involvement with one's work, as an opportunity to acquire status and avoid failure,</li><li>*However*, there is also a high degree of indiscipline.</li></ul>

EMOTIONS	<ul><li>lower levels of stress for employees,</li><li>higher levels of stress for managers,</li><li>good mental health (apparently, but also due to defense mechanisms),</li><li>a high level of happiness in children,</li><li>*However*, also lower levels of happiness, life, and work satisfaction than other modern democratic countries.</li></ul>

PERSONALITY AND RELATIONSHIPS	<ul><li>extroverted and gregarious, highly emotional, lower agreeability and conscientiousness,</li><li>transactional leaders (but focused on monitoring mistakes; fear of failure as a motivator),</li><li>*However*, defensive as a result of low self-esteem, which encourages inferiority and superiority complexes, insufficiently determined to carry things through, insufficiently autonomous, distrustful of others, cynical and skeptical, even hostile (in a controlled way), more focused on consensus than on satisfaction in the couple.</li></ul>

OTHER POSITIVE / NEGATIVE ASPECTS	<ul><li>good image of seniors,</li><li>more tolerant with minorities than their neighbors,</li><li>a willingness to fight for their own country, without considering war a good path for conflict resolution,</li><li>*However*, risky and aggressive driving, higher levels of shame and anxiety for women, and higher levels of fear in men (than Americans - n.b.).</li></ul>

Table 7. A summary of Romanian cultural traits according to Daniel David (2015)[86]

In their 2011 book *Beruflich in Rumänien* ('Doing Business in Romania'), German intercultural researchers Alexander Thomas from the University of Regensburg and his colleague Adrienne Rubatos from the Steinbeis-Hochschule Berlin paint a remarkably accurate picture of the Romanian cultural standard, very much in line with David's psychological findings. (It is interesting to look at this from a Western – particularly German – point of view.) In their assessment, the Romanian cultural profile consists of the following traits:[87]

---

[86] Source: David, D., *Psihologia poporului român*, Ed. Polirom, Bucharest, 2015, pp. 305-306, table 5.1.

[87] Thomas, A., Rubatos, A., *Beruflich in Rumänien*, Vandenhoeck & Ruprecht, Göttingen, 2011, pp. 165-167

❖ **Person orientation**:

  o people and relationships ('being on good terms with people') take priority over things, facts and results

  o need for human contact and closeness; work better with/for people they like

  o strong family ties (parents are very involved, grandparents help raise the grandchildren)

  o need and like to share and communicate; hospitable, friendly

  o take many things personally

❖ **Confrontation avoidance**

  o avoid and do not pick out conflicts, afraid not to insult and ruin relationships, often prefer to 'swallow it down'[88]

  o protecting people's feelings is more important than finding solutions

  o highly sensitive to criticism (especially from abroad)

  o fear of mistakes and consequences (embarrassment or bravado)

  o high-context, not always explicit; innuendos and non-verbal clues are important; indirect with superiors, working around negative emotions until 'they cannot hold it in any longer'

  o difficulty in presenting and defending one's position credibly

❖ **Emotionality**

  o manifestations and even outbursts of emotions are normal, even in public

---

[88] Cărtărescu, M., *Frumoasele străine*, Humanitas, 2010, pp.162-176

- o showing emotions is akin to showing interest (standoffish neutrality makes people seem unapproachable, disinterested, aloof, incomplete)
- o easily hurt or insulted, but does not last long; think with their hearts
- o restraint and sometimes reluctance; positive emotions are expressed directly, negative ones typically more indirectly (more recently, this is changing, but expressing negativity directly is still perceived as aggressive)
- o emotional arguments, subjective views often appears more important than objective criteria/data (which is often missing)[89]

❖ **Pragmatism**

- o spontaneous and intuitive approaches (the important thing is 'it works')
- o creative and individual solutions, often with few resources
- o (very) short-term thinking; life cannot really be controlled, all we have is now
- o lower regard for rules and structures ('cutting corners')
- o situational evaluations and actions, as circumstances change, approaches, plans, or solutions also change ('rules are made for people, not people for rules')
- o little respect for institutional authority and bureaucratic procedures

---

[89] A quick look at the Romanian media landscape and political debates over the past decade confirms this.

❖ **Hierarchy orientation**

- o ambivalent towards authority: outwardly - great respect, inwardly - resistance; they prefer not to depend on anyone but attempt to please to ensure future
- o superiors bear full responsibility; ambitious employees may welcome more challenging tasks to showcase their abilities
- o authoritarian (paternalistic) management style
- o person-oriented sense of responsibility, work better for and with people they like on a personal level

❖ **Fluctuating/wavering self-assuredness**

- o insecurities regarding the social position and the future; Romanians often lack self-confidence
- o vacillate between deprecation and overestimation of their country (love-hate relationship to own identity); Romanians are more comfortable in groups
- o a complex of inferiority vis-à-vis the West, Romanians sometimes tend to over-compensate
- o tough self-criticism but want to be liked by foreigners
- o self-victimization and grandiose imagery about the past and their virtues

❖ **Status orientation**

- o status symbols are important (money, car, house, brand clothing, etc. but also titles, position, connections, education, upbringing)
- o desire to catch up and be envied in terms of material gain, to have 'the latest'
- o personal sacrifice and high expenses for obtaining status symbols (big 'baroque' feasts[90], big weddings, stressful jobs, etc.)
- o tendency to categorize people according to status symbols.

Looking for answers to the question of what influences culture is a little like trying to solve the age-old chicken and egg dilemma.

Rădulescu-Motru (1937) considered hereditary, historical, and geographical factors in his explanatory narrative of the Romanian soul. He investigated the number of school drop-outs in the 1930s to validate his improvisation and lack-of-perseverance theory.[91]

R. D. Lewis (2008) views Romanian history and the country's geographical location as important determining factors that have shaped Romanian culture. In his opinion, "Romania is situated in that part of Europe which was inhabited by peasant masses, ruled for centuries by sovereign lords, clan leaders, and

---

[90] Romanian meals often consist of three or more courses (several appetizers, soup, main courses), plus desert and lots of drinks, which is considered normal hospitality/generosity in Romania; German frugality is seen as petty in comparison - see also G. Liiceanu, "Extremele culinare" in Restograf.ro, http://www.restograf.ro/gabriel-liiceanu-extremele-culinare/, 28.04.2016

[91] Rădulescu-Motru, C., *Psihologia poporului român*, Ed. Paideia, Bucharest, 1999, pp. 22-24

autocrats. They held the power of life and death over their underlings. Being themselves the law, they were above the law. They were all-powerful and went unpunished. From ancient times these people were the objects of blind and slavish worship. Ceausescu belonged to that very tradition."[92] Individualism was not only discouraged but it was also downright dangerous, and there was little to no room for assertive critical thinking (except jokes and double-talk) or private initiative. Collectivism and paternalism went hand in hand. These things are now gradually changing.

According to German researchers Alexander Thomas and Adrienne Rubatos (2011), the Romanians are greatly influenced by their Latinity and Orthodoxy. According to them, pastoral traditions whereby Romanians were alone in the mountains with their herds of sheep for months on end led to a diffuse and fluid sense of time, in stark opposition to the ambitious and highly structured lifestyle of the West. The Orthodox church also traditionally encouraged a simpler agrarian lifestyle, free of all worldly passions, in direct contact with nature and God, and Romanians yearn for this contemplative leisure to this day.[93] In western cultures, work is often hailed as a moral virtue, as a validation of a person's actions and their very life, whereas Orthodox spirituality often sees work (or, rather, toil) as a punishment imposed on men after their fall from the grace of God, as an unnatural state (the first people did not work in the Garden of Eden; paradise is without struggles or work, and

---

[92] Lewis, R.D., *Cross-Cultural Communication: A Visual Approach*, Transcreen Publications, Warnford, 2008, p. 156.
[93] Thomas, A., Rubatos, A., *Beruflich in Rumänien*, Vandenhoeck & Ruprecht, Göttingen, 2011, p. 83.

human endeavor should be focused on the spiritual, not the material; workaholism is a sign of spiritual imbalance).

Having freed themselves of the "dialectic materialism" of communism, many Romanians rediscovered their *Christian faith* and *Orthodox identity*. They also wanted freedom – often understood as the right to do anything they please how and when they please – and to make their voice heard (often, all at once). Later, the general disorder in public life as well as the high levels of uncertainty, poverty, illness, immorality, etc. led many people to distrust Parliament, become nostalgic for communism, or look for spiritual guidance, stability, and authority in the Romanian Orthodox Church (age-old rituals that give meaning, God's love and protection, closeness to absolute truth, justice, purity). In a context of muddled values, disorientation, and extreme economic distress, individualism is still unfeasible for many. Survivalism and traditionalism offer better answers.

Searching for the underlying causes of Romania's current situation and cultural standard (or rather its ambivalence), as well as its age-old norms, practices, and habits, historian Lucian Boia (2012) claims several factors can explain it:[94]

- *An impressive delay in nation-building, in establishing political structures and institutions*; the three Romanian principalities (Transylvania, Walachia, and Moldavia), located at the crossroads of many empires and foreign interests failed to produce significant texts until late into the 14th century. Here, the Middle Ages began after they had almost ended in Western Europe. The state was traditionally weak, unstable, and the people (see folk

---

[94] Boia, L., *De ce este România altfel?*, Ed. Humanitas, Bucharest, 2012, pp.7-112

ballad *Miorița*) fatalistic. The Turkish model (princes from the Fanar quarter in Istanbul, appointed by and loyal to the Sultan) depleted the country and introduced additional moral relativism; corruption and despotism abounded;

- *The marginal status of these frontier regions* led to both an extraordinary openness, receptiveness and intermingling, ethnic and linguistic synthesis, and a closed, conservative rural civilization focused on bare survival;

- *The contribution of the returning francophone elites who had studied in Paris in the mid-1800s* with a strong desire to modernize, unify, and westernize the country; the French model was adopted in politics and legislation and the first Universities, Academies, and western-style institutions were founded; oriental dress and habits were discarded. Romania fought and won a war of independence against Turkey under a German king (Carol I Hohenzollern). Subsequently, a lot of westerners settled in Romania; schools, roads, hospitals and institutions, new infrastructure, and modern architecture were built. An age of effervescence began, and Romanians began making important contributions to science (the fountain pen by Petrache Poenaru in 1827, the longest metal bridge in Europe in 1895, the Teclu burner in 1900, the first flight with a self-propelled airplane by Traian Vuia in 1906, the first bacteriology treaty by Victor Babes in 1885, etc.).

- *A chronic inferiority complex.* Romania as an independent nation-state emerged only in the late 19th century and was immediately faced with the daunting task of building a coherent common identity. Romanians realized how small and insignificant they were, always lagging behind and toeing the line of stronger powers, foreigners in their own land; a national conscience developed, attempting to compensate for this smallness. Mihai Eminescu, considered by many the most influential Romanian poet of all times, enriched the language and after his death became an icon for Romanians from all provinces;

- *Forms without substance.* A lack of know-how made imitation of western policies and institutions necessary. Combined with the difficulty of relinquishing the local old ways, this led to the incomplete reformation of patriarchal and agrarian models. The providential leader who can guide, fix and put everything in order has remained a staple of the Romanian mindset. The habit of conforming and complying with the whims of the powerful never completely disappeared;

- The *successful unification of all Romanian territories and the emergence of the Greater Romania in 1918* under a German king and his British wife (Queen Mary, granddaughter of the Queen of England and the Russian Tsar) brought new enthusiasm and hope. However, the integration of Transylvania, with its Austro-Hungarian heritage, did not go as smoothly for the Romanian elites there, who, unaccustomed to the Levantine ways of the Bucharest politicians, soon became disenchanted and marginalized. Commerce and industry grew, but not exceptionally. There was a land reform - 80% of the population continued to live in rural areas (according to the 2022 census, 46% still do). Education improved, a cultural, commercial, and industrial elite emerged. A so-called "golden age" of arts and sciences ensued, with important contributions to world culture (Blaga,

Eliade, Cioran, Ionesco, Brâncuși, Grigorescu, Tristan Tzara, Emil Racoviță, etc.);

- *The Second World War and the loss of territories.* An initial alliance with Nazi Germany, then a drastic change of course on August 2, 1944. The pendulum of history swung again, dramatically.

- *Communism.* De facto occupation by the Red Army, a purging of the elites, mass political imprisonments, communism, forced nationalization, and collectivization. The Romanians were forced to adapt, give up their property, lose their livelihoods, accept new authoritarian rulers and totalitarianism, flee, or be deported. Some, unaware of the Yalta deal, formed militias in the mountains and kept waiting for the U.S. forces to liberate Romania, which never happened. Captured political prisoners were tortured and murdered, free thought disappeared, the industry was nationalized, people had to keep a very low profile, denunciate, or steal to survive. Communist nationalism and a ridiculous cult of personality for Ceausescu were imposed on the people by the feared secret service Securitate. Critical thinking survived only under the guise of secret jokes about the regime, a coping mechanism for venting accumulated frustration. Brutal communism and forced 'patriotic work' dealt yet another blow to individualism, human trust, genuine cooperation, perseverance, prosperity, and civic involvement. Ingenious survival methods and improvisations flourished in the general penury;

- *The bloodiest anti-communist revolution in Europe (1989) and a difficult transition to democracy and capitalism.* Second-echelon communists held on to power and soon compromised the ideals of freedom, private initiative, private property, capitalism, westernization. Chaotic transition policies were implemented. Privatization was often done among acolytes and agricultural lands were not returned to the people soon enough to take advantage of the entrepreneurial euphoria after the Revolution. The violent miners' riots dramatically polarized the country, ruining Romania's image in the foreign media and sowing strife, fear, and hopelessness once again. Incomes fell sharply, while unemployment skyrocketed; birth rates decreased dramatically, health parameters deteriorated, and the country became dependent on imports. Corruption and an attraction to easy money increased. Disenchantment with politics and politicians, a distrust of businesspeople (nouveau-riche), rampant poverty, brain drain, apathy, and confusion of values (anomy) were the result.

- Misconceptions about *the Roma minority* (previously "Gypsies", a population of North Indian origin often equated with ethnic Romanians by the Western media), and their actions abroad cause great *embarrassment and anger* in Romania, deepening the complex of inferiority and shame (very stressful for an emotional Latin nation who wants to belong in 'civilized' Europe). Suspicion grew and self-confidence plummeted. Complaints about Western hypocrisy and even conspiracy theories began to circulate.

Daniel David (2015) also takes into consideration biological/genetic or environmental and policy factors (e.g., school curriculum; collectivism as a coping mechanism) to explain some psychological or cultural patterns. He considers the historical background a plausible factor but warns that connecting history to cultural developments is not yet an exact science. In his view, the underlying gregariousness and collectivism of Romanians are due to their need for security throughout history. He explains perseverance as almost futile in a region where everything is destroyed, changed, and toppled so frequently as a result of war. Human trust was not supported by the Romanians' interactions with their local and foreign masters, who attempted to control or exploit them. Strangers were often enemies and with endemic poverty the survival of one's own family was constantly an issue, so a sense of cooperation outside of one's small group did not develop. In an insecure environment, any individualism (or people standing out, doing things differently) threatened to destroy the fragile equilibrium of the group and generate strife. Indiscipline and passive-aggressive behavior were probably both a coping mechanism and the way in which the weak managed to maintain their identity, etc.[95] Survival meant constant adjustment.

Having said that, though, David also questions whether such adaptive attributes are still useful today.

Admission to NATO and the EU have increased the Romanians' sense of security and opportunity. Communism and its crimes have been officially condemned, but some people remain nostalgic for the 'safer' earlier times. The Brussels-driven justice reform, supported by a majority of Romanians, has led to the emergence of stronger *anti-corruption* institutions and progress has been made in this area.

Technological advances have reached Romania (broadband Internet speeds higher than in most Western countries, top 10 worldwide as of 2021), and freedom of movement allows approximately 3-4 million Romanians to

---

[95] David, D., *Psihologia poporului român*, Ed. Polirom, Bucharest, 2015, p.310.

work and live abroad, sending money back home and importing new ideas and approaches. The breakdown of old, collectivistic structures in the countryside, a desire to reach Western living standards as soon as possible, the influence of American pop culture, coupled with unemployment, competition, and the demise of the old safety net have prompted many Romanians to become more self-reliant and entrepreneurial (self-agency, see Trompenaars' findings on Romania which appear to confirm this). In 2016, the rate of SMEs per 1000 inhabitants in Romania (21.3) was about half of the EU average (42.7), but only slightly lower than that of Germany (27.7) and Great Britain (27.2). In 2014 and 2015, the growth rate of SME performance indicators had accelerated in Romania, with rates above the EU average. Romania also had more SMEs in the processing industries than the EU average.[96] According to STATISTA, in 2022 Romania ranked mid-range in the EU for its total number of SMEs.

Economic growth is improving, with engineering (automotive, IT), textiles, petrol, wood, and agriculture as driving forces[97], and a budding civil society is being created by young middle-class professionals and ambitious entrepreneurs. Intelligence and creativity are beginning to be rewarded and Romanians quickly embrace western trends, which they combine with original local inputs (*eclectism*). Initially, low absorption of EU funds, immature institutions, bureaucracy, and poor road infrastructure hemmed growth and for a long time Romania remained a net contributor to the EU budget. By 2022,

---

[96] Cuncea, C. in Mediafax, "România, pe ultimul loc în Europa după numărul de IMM-uri active", online edition, http://www.mediafax.ro/economic/romania-pe-ultimul-loc-in-europa-dupa-numarul-de-imm-uri-active-13773363, 28.04.2016

[97] Rosca, C. in Ziarul Financiar, "Top campioni la exporturi pe județe", online edition, http://www.zf.ro/companii/in-aproape-o-treime-din-judetele-tarii-cel-mai-mare-exportator-vine-din-industria-auto-14846958, 28.04.2016

however, this situation had been reversed, Romania having received around EUR 40 bln more than it has paid into the EU budget.

In 2014, Romania elected its first President belonging to an ethnic minority, pinning hopes on the stereotype of the rigorous German who "gets things done well". Well-educated younger generations are becoming more individualistic and better organized, demanding more accountability from government officials and employers alike. After the economic meltdown of 2008 and the ensuing austerity, wages began to rise again in 2014, industrial and construction indicators improved, the GDP rose and unemployment fell.

The economy is becoming more dynamic, and increasingly attracts foreign investment, thanks to its proximity to Western Europe and the low-priced, well-educated workforce. Bucharest, Cluj, Timisoara, Sibiu, and other cities have become ebullient start-up hubs with lively and diverse cultural scenes. *Social media* has become a force in elections or corruption scandals. In 2015, for the first time, an INSCOP survey showed that the National Anti-Corruption Department had surpassed the Church in terms of popular trust (61.2% vs. 56.3%).[98] *Digitalization* is seen as a chance against arbitrary interpretations and corruption, as well as an opportunity for more lucrative business models and less bureaucracy. It also changes the way people spend their time, interact and communicate. According to Mercury Research, as of 2016, Romanians used to spend a lot of time online and watching television (87% watched TV every day; average TV consumption = 3.3 hours/day during

---

[98] Digi24, "Sondaj: A crescut încrederea românilor în Preşedinţie şi a scăzut încrederea în Biserică", http://www.digi24.ro/Stiri/Digi24/Actualitate/Social/INSCOP+A+scazut+increderea+in+Biseri ca, 28.04.2016

the week; most viewed: news, films, music, and entertainment - in this order).[99] Social media and streaming services are now biting into that market.

Up to this point, everyday life shows that, in Romania, informal networks (someone who knows someone who knows someone who...) continue to remain more reliable sources of information and assistance than official structures. Social status is very important because it affects the supportive networks one can build and the clout one amasses. Time is willy-nilly becoming more structured. Western pop culture is introducing new standards and expectations.

What will Romanian culture look like in another 25 years, if these trends continue? That is an exciting question.

3.3. Self-perception, hetero-perception, and stereotypes

3.3.1. Self-stereotypes of Romanians (how the Romanians see themselves)

When asked how they would characterize their own culture as part of a survey run by David et al, Romanians answered, in this order:[100]

POSITIVE TRAITS

- hospitable, welcoming (warm, friendly) (>20%)

- hard-working (10%)

- intelligent

---

[99] Stanca, A. in Realitatea.net, "Studiu: Cât de mult se uită românii la televizor şi ce programe preferă", online edition, http://www.realitatea.net/cat-de-mult-de-uita-romanii-la-televizor-si-ce-programe-prefera_1795074.html, 28.04.2016

[100] David, D., *Psihologia poporului român*, Ed. Polirom, Bucharest, 2015, pp. 280-285, study no. 2

NEGATIVE TRAITS

- negligent, indifferent (cynical, skeptical) (>20%)
- mean-spirited (10%)
- corrupt.

A CURS survey from 2005 brought to light the following self-stereotype of Romanians:

POSITIVE TRAITS

- hospitable (19%)
- hard-working (10%)
- inventive (10%)
- religious (9%)

NEGATIVE TRAITS

- negligent (10%)
- divided (10%)
- frivolous (not serious) (10%)
- selfish (9%).

According to Dâncu et al. (2014), in a different survey, Romanians believe the following about themselves:

POSITIVE TRAITS

- welcoming (67%)
- hard-working (47%)
- decent, good-hearted (40%)
- intelligent (29%)
- religious (17%).

A different methodology used by Dâncu and Orban (2015) portrays the Romanians as hospitable, smart and resourceful, and intelligent, but also – at the opposite end of the spectrum – as boring and lazy.

The interesting thing to notice is that honesty, which appeared as an important self-attributed trait of Romanians in surveys dating from 1988 and 1993, begins to lose ground in the new economic environment (transition to capitalism), and by 2005-2007 disappears completely. A self-perception study of Romanians run exclusively on participants from Bucharest has the following results: hard-working, dishonest, intelligent, and welcoming, but also poor and naive!

There are some differences in self-perception among the three major historical regions. For Transylvania, the results of David's survey were: hard-working (>20%), slow (10%), hospitable and civilized. In Wallachia, the results read: resourceful (>20%), impulsive (10%), arrogant. And in Moldavia, the order is: negligent (>20%), hospitable (10%), hard-working.

Generally, Romanians perceive themselves as warm and intelligent but undisciplined. In other words, they perceive themselves more positively in terms of personality and more negatively in terms of actual behavior.[101] Hungarians see us as patriotic and well-adjusted, religious, welcoming and good-hearted, but also hypocritical (Dâncu et al. 2014). Italians see Romanians as rather lazy (PEW Research Center, 2012) and in Western Europe Romanians have often been associated with a lack of thoroughness (or conscientiousness) and with some types of antisocial behavior.

---

[101] David, D., *Psihologia poporului român*, Ed. Polirom, Bucharest, 2015, p. 311

According to an INSCOP survey from April 2016, 85.4% of Romanians had a positive image of their country.[102] Although Romanians perceive themselves as warm and welcoming, to Westerners they often appear suspicious and cynical. "Undisciplined" appears both in the self-stereotype and in the hetero-stereotype. What Romanians consider to be a "positive personality" is seen as very high emotionality (extroversion) and low conscientiousness by the Western world. And whereas Romanians see themselves as balanced between vertical collectivism with a low distribution of power, and selfishness (individualism, everybody wants power within the group), Westerners often see collectivism, gregariousness, and lack of consistency.[103]

An article by German-language newspaper *Die Welt* (2013) also mentions a certain complex of inferiority as central to the present-day Romanian psyche. "‹*We are so small and insignificant*› *(...)* For centuries now, the Romanian has been feeling humiliated by foreigners, threatened by great powers, instrumentalized and exploited."[104] Indeed, ‹*While we were here fending off the Turks, the West was building its huge cathedrals*› is a beloved refrain in Romania. Also, Romanians resent being put on the same level as the Roma minority (a nomadic population of North Indian origin probably belonging to the caste of the "untouchables" there, which fled towards Europe

---

[102] INSCOP, "Barometrul Adevărul despre România - Simpatie țări", April 2016, p. 4

[103] David, D., *Psihologia poporului român*, Ed. Polirom, Bucharest, 2015, pp. 313-314, table 5.2.

[104] Scheida, W. in Die Welt, "Heikles Selbstbild - Die Rumänen und ihr Gefühl, wertlos zu sein", online edition, http://www.welt.de/debatte/kommentare/article113852181/Die-Rumaenen-und-ihr-Gefuehl-wertlos-zu-sein.html, 28.04.2016

in the 14th century[105] and is still largely unintegrated), which they prefer to call Gypsies (*țigani*) for fear of being completely confused with them abroad.

3.3.2. Stereotypes about Germans in Romania

According to David (2015), the most common stereotype about Germans in Romania is that they are "organized". (This may seem like very little, but if we think about it, good organization almost necessarily entails rationality, seriousness, and structure, which in turn entails planning ahead, rigorous scheduling, a separation of tasks and spheres, and not giving in to fleeting emotions.) The Romanians prefer the British, the Americans, and the French (in this order), then the Germans. The Hungarians and the Russians rank among the lowest in their preferences.

According to the same INSCOP survey on country sympathies in April 2016, Germany ranked 11th, with 73.7% of Romanians having a positive image (liking) of Germany. However, when asked which country they consider to be Romania's main ally for purposes of national security, Romanians ranked Germany second after the USA (9.2% for Germany as opposed to 49.7% for the USA).[106]

Other stereotypes about Germans in Romania and the Romanian Diaspora are that they are serious, civilized, cold, distant, rigid (sticklers for details and procedures), thrifty/parsimonious, fair and honest, thorough (high-quality products), effective and efficient.

---

[105] Djuvara, N., *O scurtă istorie a românilor povestită celor tineri*, Ed. Humanitas, Bucharest, 2008, pp.76-77

[106] INSCOP, "Barometrul Adevărul despre România - Simpatie țări", April 2016, p. 5

A German travel website describes the situation as follows: "Romanians (...) view the Germans in particular as self-confident, intelligent, competent, strict and disciplined."[107] The same source goes on to mention that "culturally, Romanians (...) see themselves as hospitable, warm and affectionate. On the other hand, they consider for instance the Germans to be rather cold, less affectionate, and less welcoming. Romanians have long been inculcated with the concept of conviviality (hospitality) and with the idea that they traditionally work hard. They believe the Germans also work hard, and for this reason, feel that they are in a way related."

Alexander Thomas and Adrienne Rubatos (2011) note that "Romanians believe that Germans miss out on so much in life with their seriousness, and will gladly show them that other ways are possible"[108].

3.3.3. Self-stereotypes of Germans (how the Germans see themselves)

According to a GfK survey from 2006, the Germans view themselves mostly as:[109]

- hard-working and conscientious (industrious, diligent, assiduous): 23%

- orderly, well-organized, meticulous, pedantic: 13.1%

- punctual: 13.1%

- clean and tidy: 12.5%

---

[107]Frank, B., Mietwagen-Auskunft.de, http://www.mietwagen-auskunft.de/rumaenien/mentalitaet/, 28.04.2016

[108] Thomas, A., Rubatos, A., *Beruflich in Rumänien*, Vandenhoeck & Ruprecht, Göttingen, 2011, p. 82

[109] Source: GfK Nurnberg e.V., "Was ist deutsch", 2006 (http://www.nbaservice.com/europa_image_deutschland.html), 06.04.2016

Interestingly enough, this point of view is not entirely shared by other Europeans, who associate the Germans with:

- orderly, well-organized, meticulous, pedantic: 9.8%

- war, in general: 8.8%

- beer: 5.0%

- hard work and conscientiousness (diligence): 4.3%.

A recent FORSA study, however, shows that with regard to WWII German perceptions are changing, with Germans feeling that they have made enough amends for the past. Rather, Germans today are beginning to recast themselves as victims of the Nazi regime and the war.[110] They also consider themselves very ecologically-minded (insisting on separating the trash, clean air regulations, belief in bio-products, etc.), and view themselves as a leading force in environmentalism worldwide (if we are to believe the evening news).

Even informal street interviews conducted in Berlin and posted on YouTube show both young and older Germans describing themselves as: "punctual", "accurate", "precise", "honest", "proper and solid", "organized", "strict", "upfront and straight forward", "controlled", "sticklers to rules", "perfectionists", "hard-working", "concrete", "structured", "always having a plan", "serious, not funny", needing "fences and frames for everything".[111]

---

[110] Charter, D. in Times Europe, "Germans begin to recast themselves as victims of the Nazis", online edition, http://www.thetimes.co.uk/tto/news/world/europe/article4426313.ece, 28.04.2016

[111] see TheYafaShow, YouTube, https://www.youtube.com/watch?v=DftvAq3UhzE, 06.06.2016

3.3.4. Stereotypes about Romanians in Germany

According to a 2015 newspaper article on BlastingNews, Romanians (and Bulgarians) were still struggling with a very negative perception in Germany. "Migrants from Romania and Bulgaria have always had to fight prejudice. The stereotype about these migrants can be described as follows: an unemployed illiterate who steals or sends his children and family on the streets to beg, and who comes to Germany to make a nice living off the German state and welfare system, mainly by cheating. But these Romanian and Bulgarian immigrants are often equated with the approximately 6 million Roma people from the region. (...) For instance, the Roma building in Duisburg Rheinhausen is often used as a typical example of Romanian immigrants. (...) In reality, a closer look reveals that Romanians and Bulgarians are, on average, considerably better qualified than most other groups of immigrants to Germany."[112] Many Germans are still quite unaware of the brain drain happening in Romania, with some of the best and brightest young professionals (engineers, doctors, nurses, etc.) leaving the country for the West.

Other stereotypes about Romanians circulating in Germany are or have been at some point:

---

[112] Richter, M. in BlastingNews, "Rumänen und Bulgaren, Sozialschmarotzer oder deutscher Wirtschaftsmotor", online edition, http://de.blastingnews.com/politik/2015/06/rumanen-und-bulgaren-sozialschmarotzer-oder-deutscher-wirtschaftsmotor-00423879.html, 28.04.2016

- good IT people; both low-level workers and doctors/nurses/engineers are well integrated on the German labor market (almost half a million of them already by the end of 2021, according to a FAZ article[113]

- poorest country in the EU (it is not, it is second poorest – which to Romanians makes a world of difference – but it has regions perfectly within the EU average, and in 2022 Bucharest had reached 164% of the EU average)

- one of the most corrupt countries in the EU (Transparency International's *Corruption Perception Index 2022* lists Bulgaria, Hungary, and Romania as the most corrupt among EU Member States. In 2015, Romania was tied with Greece, and scored better than Italy[114]); *everything* and *everyone* must be corrupt (the Romanians themselves see politicians, members of Parliament, policemen and other public officials as most corrupt)

- occasionally, a distrust of all Romanian credentials and documents (school certificates, driving licenses since they must have been "bought with money") - except for engineers

- nature (bears, wolves) and fascinating villages stuck in time.

Older Germans also recall how humanely they were treated as prisoners of war in Romania, but their knowledge of the country ends with Ceaușescu and the Black Sea.

---

[113] Carstens, P., Frankfurter Allgemeine Zeitung, 31.12.2021, https://www.faz.net/aktuell/politik/inland/rumaenen-und-bulgaren-oft-erfolgreich-am-deutschen-arbeitsmarkt-17709318.html

[114] Transparency International, "Corruption Perception Index 2015", published in 2016. Transparency International, "Corruption Perception Index 2022", published in 2023.

As far as prejudices go, many Germans believe all Romanians are "beggars", "thieves", poorly qualified, here to take their jobs[115], that they come only to take advantage of the social system, that they should not complain or express negative opinions, but "be grateful that they are allowed to stay and enjoy German living standards".

A 2014 article published by a long-time Romanian immigrant in the German newspaper *Die Zeit* sketches the prejudice that even well-adjusted Romanian immigrants are facing in Germany, "Every time I tell a German about my origins, there is an unpleasant moment. (...) I suppose all immigrants from poor countries make this experience when they talk about their origins in Germany. (...)."[116]

The stigma of poverty, associated almost automatically with vice, corruption and theft, deceitful social tourism, prostitutes, and Hartz IV recipients is still very much in place in Germany concerning Romanians. Even reports about Romania having one of the lowest unemployment rates in the EU, successful career women, etc. are written in a note of exoticism[117] as if one can hardly believe this of Romania. The cliché of Romania as a backward, 'backwater' country is hard to uproot.

Germans traveling to Romania on business often lament the "too pragmatic and volatile solutions, a work rhythm in spurts, or the impulsive and

---

[115] von Stockert, C. in Frankfurter Neue Presse, "Wie falsch Vorurteile gegen Rumänen sind - Intoleranz und billiges Gemüse", online edition, http://www.fnp.de/rhein-main/dasprojektjungezeitung/Intoleranz-und-billiges-Gemuese;art11422,1851082, 13.02.2016
[116] Mayer, C. in Die Zeit, "Wie ein Bürger dritter Klasse", online edition, http://www.zeit.de/gesellschaft/2014-01/integration-deutschland-rumaenien, 28.04.2016
[117] idem.

chaotic driving behavior of Romanians"[118], their emotionality, and the communication for communication's sake (without getting to the point; in reality, this is Thun von Schulz "self-revelation" side of communication, very important to Romanians).

German businesspeople sometimes tend to equate the Romanian ethos with the Italians, but while its expressiveness and loquacity are undoubtedly of Latin descent, there is also another side to Romanians, the quiet, introverted, and contemplative side that has more in common with the Slavic or Greek melancholy.

3.4. Conclusions

While stereotypes are certainly necessary and useful in simplifying reality and in helping us navigate a complex environment, they are often emotional generalizations that can lead to even more negativity, discrimination, and even conflict.

Stereotypes may contain some grain of truth about the people being stereotyped, but they speak volumes about the people doing the stereotyping – about their benchmarks, interpretation filters (expectations), own patterns of action, and willingness to accept otherness.

It is, therefore, my deepest conviction that a rational description of both cultures from a variety of angles, as well as a rational examination of the causes, historical evolutions, and the external manifestations of the deeper

---

[118] Thomas, A., Rubatos, A., *Beruflich in Rumänien*, Vandenhoeck & Ruprecht, Göttingen, 2011, p. 82

cultural profile, can greatly benefit the discussion and can set the stage for improved mutual understanding.

The most salient and valuable point we can derive from our analysis so far is that, to a large extent, international models, national research from within each of the two cultures, self-perception, and hetero-perception all converge to form similar pictures. The fact that, applied to each culture, all these different approaches and criteria confirm pretty much the same set of values, suggests that we are indeed in the presence of two valid and coherent cultural profiles (or standards).

At this point, if we summarize and compile the findings of the international models of cultural analysis (external point of view), as well as those of the German and Romanian national standards (self-perception, self-analysis) to delineate the two cultural profiles in lay terms, the overall picture we get is the following (see Table 7 on the next page).

Please keep in mind though that these results are generalizations, and that categorical thinking can also give rise to prejudice – so take them with a grain of salt!

Category of cultural analysis	GERMANY	ROMANIA
TIME	- a strict sense of time, rigorous scheduling, linearity - medium and long-term orientation	- a more fluid sense of time, multi-tasking - short-term orientation
SPACE	- distance and discretion - separation of life spheres, larger personal space bubbles	- closeness and human contact - the overlapping of life spheres, sharing - tactile (touching, kissing)
COMMUNICATION AND EMOTION	- low-context, assertive, explicit, direct, detailed communication, confrontational - neutral, formal, and self-controlled - almost exclusively objective criteria (originating from reason/the brain)	- high-context, implicit and often indirect; non-verbal clues; confrontation avoidance - highly emotional, less formal - subjective criteria (originating from the heart) are important
STRUCTURE AND ACTION	- structure-oriented, rule-driven, task-oriented, linear - thorough and efficient, due process, obey the procedure	- creative, resourceful, spontaneous, flexible - relative disregard for regulations and lengthy

Category of cultural analysis	GERMANY	ROMANIA
	- restrained and disciplined - self-confident - clear and strict regulations and procedures to limit uncertainty	processes; dislike of rigid and pompous officialdom; ambivalence towards authority; suspicion - restrained, undisciplined - fluctuating confidence (in both self and others) - networks (family, friends, acquaintances), rumors, tradition, and faith to deal with uncertainty
HUMAN RELATIONSHIPS AND COMPETITIVENESS	-things-oriented, performance-oriented, masculine; trust is task-based[119] - individualistic - status-oriented (academic titles, seniority, competence, car, house)	- person-oriented, feminine, skeptical, trust is relationship-based -gregarious (a mixture of collectivism and individualism) - status-oriented (money, brand clothes, position, connections, car, house, travels, etc.)

---

[119] Meyer, E., *The Culture Map*, Public Affairs, New York, 2014, p. 171

Category of cultural analysis	GERMANY	ROMANIA
POWER	- hierarchical, but power is more evenly distributed, and regulated more equitably - more consensual[120], participative, and autonomous	- hierarchical - more paternalistic, less inclusive; contrasts and deference; expect strong but fair leader, less cooperation - top-down, competition-oriented, self-protective, but also group-protective in certain contexts
ENVIRON-MENT	- control environment and external circumstances (internal locus of control)	- controlled by environment and external circumstances (external locus of control)

Table 8. A summary of German vs. Romanian cultural profiles along with the most important categories of cultural analysis

We can now proceed to investigate how these cultural traits are reflected in language and communication, how language itself influences culture, and derive some practical guidelines for cross-cultural interactions.

---

[120] idem, p.150

4. Germans and Romanians Talking. Culture Reflected in Speech - Patterns of Communication and Linguistic Expression

I consider language to be both a relative determinant of thought processes (and therefore of culture) and an outward manifestation of culture. It is my conviction that language and communication patterns and styles both create and reflect culture, and that their analysis can help bridge cultural gaps and create guides for better understanding and mutually beneficial interactions.

4.1. German language vs. Romanian language. A brief linguistic analysis

German is a West Germanic language belonging to the family of Indo-European languages and spoken by approximately 95 million people worldwide. Its vocabulary is estimated at anything between 300,000 and 500,000 words. The German dictionary by the Grimm brothers (1852-1971) contains around 450,000. Of these, there are many Latin and Greek imports, and a few are from French and English - but usually, even neologisms and imports are translated into German. With official variants in Austria, Switzerland, and Germany, it is a pluricentric language, with a broad range of dialects. It is rather regular in structure and has three different genders (feminine: 46%, masculine: 34%, neutral: 20% - according to *Duden - Die Deutsche Rechtschreibung* (2009).

On the other hand, Romanian is an Eastern Romance language belonging to the family of Indo-European languages and spoken by approximately 24 million people. Its vocabulary is estimated at anything between 200,000 and

600,000 words, with lots of synonyms and homonyms. *DEXonline*, the online version of the Romanian Explanatory Dictionary, currently stands at 717,082 definitions, but it is unclear how many are repetitions or derived forms.[121] Over the centuries, Romanian has received considerable inputs from Slavic languages, French, Turkish, German, English, and Hungarian. R. D. Lewis (2008) goes as far as to call it a "hybrid language", richer than both Slavic and Latin. Romanian is based on Vulgar Latin, introduced by Roman colonizers after the annexation of Dacia by Trajan in 105-106 A.D. It is the official language in Romania, the Republic of Moldova, the Vojvodina region in Serbia, and Mount Athos. It is a surprisingly unitary language (slight variations in vocabulary and pronunciation do not warrant calling regional variants dialects), also called Daco-Romanian to distinguish it from its relatives Aromanian, Megleno-Romanian, and Istro-Romanian. Generally, Romanian is considered to be among the most irregular of Romance languages.

Here's a quick summary of German and Romanian grammar:

---

[121] as of 06.04.2016.

Language / Parameter	German	Romanian
Declensions (cases of nouns)	**4** (*Nominativ, Akkusativ, Genitiv, Dativ*)	**5** (*Nominativ, Acuzativ, Genitiv, Dativ, Vocativ*)
Genders of nouns	**3** (*Fem., Mask., Neutrum*)	**3** (*fem., masc., neutru* - but in reality neuter is not a separate gender; it behaves as masculine in the singular and as feminine in the plural)
Categories of verbs	**2** (weak and strong)	**5** (verbs ending in "a", "ea", "e", "i", und "î")
Tenses of verbs	**6** (*Präsens, Perfekt, Präteritum, Plusquamperfekt, Futur I, Futur II*)	**9** (*prezent, imperfect, perfect compus, mai mult ca perfect, perfect simplu, viitor I, viitor II, viitor popular, viitor anterior*)
Modes of verbs	**5**	**8**

Language / Parameter	German	Romanian
	(*Infinitiv, Indikativ, Imperativ, Konjunktiv, Partizip*)	(*infinitiv, indicativ, conjunctiv, condiţional-optativ, imperativ, participiu, supin, gerunziu*)
Definite articles	*der, die, das* (as separate articles before the noun)	*+a, +ul /-l/-le (sg.), +le, +i (pl.)* (as terminations at the end of the noun)

Table 9. A brief comparative analysis of German and Romanian grammar structures

While German is very precise, rigorous, and structured, Romanian, due to its complex, irregular and rich grammar allows very nuanced and ambiguous (ambivalent) forms of expression. Romanian also allows impressive flexibility. There are short forms for many words (such as: *azi* = *astăzi* = today, *asta* = *aceasta* = this, *aia* = *aceea* = that, *e* = *este* = is, numerals above 10, etc.), the personal pronoun is most often dropped before the verb (as it is unnecessary, the person can be distinguished from the terminations of the conjugated verb), the order of the words in the sentence is not predetermined, and there are three different forms of the personal pronoun in accusative and dative (the stressed form, the unstressed unbound, and the unstressed bound form)!

The Romanian language uses a lot of open vowels (a, e, o, ă), and has a lot of diphthongs and triphthongs (groups of two or three vowels which are pronounced together): *oa, ea, ioa, ia, ie,* etc. For instance, *şcoală* - şcoa-lă (Schule), *Ioana* - Ioa-na (Johanna), *rău/rea* (schlecht, mask. und fem.)

Another interesting aspect is that of weekdays. While German has translated the names of days from Latin and innovated for "Wednesday" (which is *Mittwoch* or "midweek" instead of Mercurii), Romanian has kept all of the initial Latin names, except those for Saturday (which became *Sâmbătă* probably in accordance with the Jewish Sabbat), and Sunday (which became *Duminică*, from Dominus – the day of the Lord), perhaps an indicator of early Christianization.

The German language is very much based on nouns, and it constantly creates more nouns by the composition of two or more other words. They are thus both extremely complex and very streamlined. This peculiarity allows for impersonal and neutral expression since unlike verbs they do not have to be conjugated in a certain person. Passive voice is often used. As Mark Twain observed in his book *A Tramp abroad (1880)*, some German nouns are so long, they have their own perspective. German has strict rules about cases and word order in a sentence (verb always in the second position in the main sentence, and always at the end in a subordinated clause). Verbs have prefixes that must be separated from the verb and placed at the end of the sentence, which requires very focused logical thinking and accuracy in crafting the phrase, as well as patient listening skills till the very end, as this prefix can make the difference between two antonyms and thus completely change the meaning of the sentence!

In Romanian, there are no composite nouns. Complex concepts are not created by fusing two or more nouns, but by means of prepositions. There are, however, many more groups of verbs. Romanian has imported many words from the cultures it came into contact with and has not been as eager to translate them, but rather they entered the vocabulary in their original form and were "Romanized" only in pronunciation and spelling (for example, *ciorap* - from the Turkish "çorab", *muncă* - from the Hungarian "munka", *ambuteiaj* - from the French "embouteillage", *șaibă* - from the German "Scheibe", etc.).

There are, thus, many synonyms from many different centuries and with many different etymologies. Because grammar rules are complex, with many exceptions, and many different word orders are possible and accepted, with adjectives that have to conform in gender with the noun in both singular and plural, and many homonyms, Romanian lends itself to subtle rhetoric, double meanings, long, winding sentences, fantastic imagery and catchy turns of phrase.

One quite exciting aspect is that of masculinity/femininity manifested in language, and here we cannot avoid talking about *Vaterland* vs. *Patria mumă*. The German term for country (as is that for house) is neuter (*das Land*, *Vaterland* = fatherland), while in Romanian, although derived from the Latin "pater" (father), it is feminine (house, *casa*, is also feminine). Adding *mumă* (archaic for mother) to *patria*, actually creates an oxymoron, another Romanian paradox! This is also an indication of Romanian humor and mockery (see 4.4.1. German vs. Romanian humor and jokes).

4.2. Bring on those ballads! German vs. Romanian popular expression and folklore

4.2.1. German vs. Romanian foundational myths, tales, songs, dances, religious beliefs

The German ethnicity and a "German people" emerged in the Middle Ages; the history of the German nation is considered to start with Charlemagne (Holy Roman Emperor, 768-814) and the division of his Empire among his grandchildren.[122] As descendants of the Germanic tribes of the North German plains and southern Scandinavia, early Germans must have been influenced by Norsk pagan mythology, including venerations of trees (oak tree, Yule tree), solstice feasts, etc. which are still discernible in German popular culture to this day (decoration of Christmas tree, love of nature and forests, *Maibaum*, summer solstice celebrations with bonfires, etc.) although integrated into the Christian traditions.

German folklore retained some Northern myths, such as Holda, the patron of spinning, water spirits or sirens such as Lorelei, spirits of the water, the *Weisse Frauen*, elves, dwarfs, and kobolds. Christian holiday traditions, especially in Bavaria, include pagan characters such as the *Krampus* (frightening half-man, half-goat who scares bad children into behaving before Christmas), the Easter Bunny, the *Walpurgisnacht*. Folklore characters include the Piper of Hamelin, the prankster Till Eulenspiegel, the Musicians of Bremen, and the fairy

---

[122] Anonymous, DerWeg.org, https://www.derweg.org/deutschland/geschichte/, 06.04.2016

tales collected by the Grimm Brothers often include: witches, vane stepmothers in search of eternal youth and beauty (Snow White, Rapunzel); curses on young princesses (Snow White, Sleeping Beauty); parents either incarcerating their children (*Rapunzel*) or casting them out into the woods (Hänsel and Gretel); orphaned but virtuous girls (Cinderella) who marry into nobility; stupidity (The Wise Eloise), coupled with good-nature and freedom from all worry (*Hans im Glück*); clever and skilled craftsmen or peasant's daughters (The Valiant Little Tailor, The Miller's Daughter); imps that demand retribution (*Rumpelstiltzchen*); dwarfs; evil wolves (Little Red Riding Hood, The Wolf, and the Seven Young Kids); other wood creatures, as well as frogs (The Frog King), golden geese, cats (Puss in Boots), etc.

Possibly the most famous German folk creation is the Song of the Niebelungen, an epic poem that tells the story of the dragon-slayer Siegfried at the court of the Burgundians, and of his wife Kriemhild who avenged him after he was murdered. This legend, of which the earliest manuscript dates back to the 13th century, includes oral traditions about historic events and characters from the fifth and sixth century A.D. and contains pre-Christian heroic motifs. It is a large and tragic work in singable stanzas about adventure and heroic battle, feudal society, nobility, court life, honor and love, gender roles and constraints, envy, intrigues, rank, and posthumous fame, murder and violent death, revenge, and ultimately disintegration. Lasting joy and happiness are not possible in the absence of honor and love.

Folk songs include many Christmas carols and other songs for religious and traditional holidays, marching songs (these include brass instruments, alphorns, violins, and accordions), and children's songs. Folk dances include many marches and polkas, relatively monotonous and even-tempered, with easy steps, sometimes with some shrieking and applauding. In terms of religion, Germans are mostly Catholic (in the South) and Protestant (in the North), and the Reformation movement played a major role in their culture, etching its indelible mark.

Oktoberfest festivities, *"Dult"*, or church patron saint celebrations in catholic Germany and Austria often entail tents filled with people squeezed into each other tightly on wooden benches, consuming large quantities of beer, singing and dancing in unison, in complete contrast to their 'normal' everyday persona – an almost orgiastic event. Thus, the Germans' need for human contact finds its outlet at predetermined intervals, when they discard inhibitions and restraint. Older people in the villages still observe their "regulars' table" (Stammtisch) ritual. Religiosity is low – almost 40% of German no longer belong to a Church.[123] By comparison, the 2011 census conducted in Romania shows that only 0.21% of the population declared themselves atheists or without religion! (The 2022 census saw those numbers almost triple, but the percentage remains low.)

The Romanians trace their origins back to the Dacians (or *"geto-daci"*, a Thracian people situated around and to the North of the lower course of the Danube) and the Roman legions that conquered parts of Dacia under Emperor Trajan. Very soon, there was an ethnic and linguistic synthesis, and the language became Romanian (with roots in Vulgar Latin). Even before that, ports on the Black Sea in present-day Dobrudja (Tomis) were populated by Greek

---

[123] Eicken, J., Schmitz-Veltin, A., "Die Entwicklung der Kirchenmitglieder in Deutschland", Statistisches Bundesamt, 2010, p. 578

merchants, and Hellenism remained an important influence. Waves of migrations later added Slavic and Hungarian influences. As of the 17th century, Turkish influences became a significant force to the south of the Carpathians.

For most of their history, the Romanians lived in several different principalities (or three historical regions: Transylvania, Wallachia, and Moldavia). Despite this separation, they doggedly held on to their common language, religion, and traditions. With the Eastern Roman Empire enduring after the decline of the Western Roman Empire, the medieval Romanian states remained close to Constantinople, which allowed greater independence of local churches and a less dogmatic approach. After the Great Schism between the Eastern and Western Churches, Romanians remained Orthodox. After the 10th century, Transylvania gradually became part of the Hungarian kingdom and later of the Austro-Hungarian Empire.

After the fall of Constantinople to the Turks, Wallachia and Moldavia remained autonomous but under Turkish suzerainty and fought numerous wars against the Ottoman Empire. "Fighting to protect our country and the Christian faith" is very much part of the narrative. Stephen the Great, Prince of Moldavia (1457-1504) was named "Athlete of Christianity" by the Pope and built a church or monastery after each victory. The most famous of the painted monasteries of Bucovina is the Voroneț, World Heritage Site. He was recently sanctified by the Romanian Orthodox Church. Other rulers/princes who became myths of Romanian valor include Neagoe Basarab and Negru Vodă (considered the "founding fathers" of the kingdom of Wallachia), Mircea the Old, Michael the Brave, and Vlad the Impaler who, in the Romanian psyche, signifies honesty and rule of law through authoritarianism. Constantin

Brâncoveanu, accused of treason and beheaded by the Turks because he would not recant his Christian faith became a symbol of the ultimate sacrifice for country and faith.

Modernization came in the mid-1800s when Romanian elites in Wallachia and Moldavia imported French culture and brought in Charles of Hohenzollern, a German prince. After the Second World War, communism was imposed with brutal methods, while the country was the facto under Red Army occupation. The communist regime later veered into blatant nationalism, authoritarianism, and a cult of personality.

Religious beliefs have always played an important role in the cultural evolution of Romanians. The Dacians were themselves monotheistic (veneration of Zamolxis) and practiced human sacrifice, so Christianity caught on very quickly (according to tradition, St. Andrew christianized Dobrudja in the first century after Jesus Christ). However, remnants of agrarian myths (*Plugușorul* - The Little Plow, on Dec. 31st), fertility dances (*Călușarii*), a belief in the "undead" (*vârcolaci*), and of pre-Christian festivals (*mărțișor* - on March 1st), the dance of the bear and the goat at the end of December and beginning of January, the Roman "calendae" that became the *colinde* (the tradition of going from house to house on Christmas Eve spreading good wishes and singing carols) survived and were incorporated into the new Christian traditions.

Romanian folk tales (*basme*) have to do with: royal infertility and magic impregnations which sooner or later demand their price (*Pipăruș Petru*, *Tinerețe fără bătrânețe și viață fără de moarte* – Youth Without Old Age and Life Without Death); kings and queens who make special promises in a desperate attempt to conceive or to appease children; the youngest of three princes ("*prâslea*") having to undertake a journey of initiation containing a series of Herculean tasks (usually three) to bring back a valuable/magic object, to attain a goal, get a wife or a kingdom (*Harap-Alb, Prâslea cel voinic şi merele de aur* - The Burly Young Prince and The Golden Apples, Aleodor Împărat), and who succeeds with the help of apparently insignificant animals and other animated natural forces that the hero/heroine had previously helped/protected (ants, bees, magic winged horses, birds, fountains, trees, female dogs, roosters). These heroes usually have to defeat monstrous anthropomorphic villains such as

- *zmeu* (dragon - masculine),

- *scorpia, ghionoaia* (a type of Hydra with several heads and a terrible temper - feminine),

- *muma pădurii* (the mother of the forest), *muma zmeului* (the mother of the dragon),

or fulfill the whims of brides or of the powerful. In these tales, the concept of a quest, endurance, help from friends is omnipresent. Heroes have to measure up to supernatural evil forces, but wise animals (the father's winged horse), good fairies, or extraordinary individuals (*Harap-Alb*) help the good-hearted and valiant young hero. There is a belief throughout that you cannot manage it alone, but if you do good, good will happen to you, you will be repaid by higher forces.

Other tales include a king's three daughters (*Ileana Sânziana*), of which the youngest does a son's deeds to save her father's kingdom, and succeeds by engaging the help of her father's old and experienced horse who again turns out to have magical powers and lots of knowledge about the ways of the world.

The horse looks old and weak but is rejuvenated and invigorated through a diet of cinder and ashes (reminiscent of the periods of preparation before important religious holidays). The world outside is described as sunny and inebriatingly beautiful. Bad weather, dense woods, dragon-fighting appear as tests. Strong winds are the breath of monsters following the hero/heroine. Natural parents are portrayed as very affectionate, even the dragon's mother is glad and grateful when the hero/heroine spares her son. Sf. Vineri (Holy Friday) appears quite often as an old wise woman who separates good from bad characters and forces them to show their true colors.

There are good fairies (*zâne bune, ursitoare bune*, good deities), or bad/mad fairies (*ursitoare rele*) - they appear at the child's crib to wish it a good/troubled life, or during the hero's initiating journey, trying to derail him from his quest.

Other folk stories have to do with peasants, crushing poverty, greedy old stepmothers, virtuous and hard-working peasants' daughters, lazy and mean daughters of the peasant's new wife. The message is that of modesty and hard work (*Fata babei și fata moșului* – The Old Woman's Daughter and The Old Man's Daughter), frugality, deliverance from poverty (*Punguța cu doi bani* - The Little Purse and The Two Gold Coins), stupidity in commercial undertakings or in everyday life coupled with resourcefulness in face of the Devil (*Dănilă Prepeleac* - who is a kind of *Hans im Glück*, but wittier than the devil himself when pressed for his life). Other themes are life without death and youth without old age disturbed by pangs of longing (*dor*) for one's parents and home, cosmic projections, camaraderie, and brotherhood in arms (*frați de sânge* - blood brothers). Research shows Romanian stories contain more positive emotions and less negative emotions compared to those of other nations (see Chapter 3.2, page 50).

One of the most significant oral folk creations of the Romanians is *Miorița* (The Little Ewe), a philosophical ballad that tells the story of a shepherd whose life is threatened by two greedy rivals. One of his sheep has magical powers and warns him of his partners' evil intentions, urging him to take precautions, but the young shepherd sees little point in that and is more concerned with the details of his burial and his mother's pain. This has been interpreted as serene resignation, creative death, fatalism: the peace of his soul as he prepares to die, as well as coming up with a cheerful explanation for his disappearance (marriage to a celestial queen) to spare his mother the pain is more important. He instructs the ewe to bury him in nature, with his beloved flute pipe, and to break the news gently to his mother. There is wistfulness and unconditional acceptance of one's faith and a search for the reunification with the whole, the universal; a yearning for the oceanic feeling that existed before individuation. What little proactive behavior the shepherd musters is directed towards his loved ones, not toward material possessions. The ballad is filled with pastoral, metaphysical, and cosmic elements and the mountain landscape is described as very peaceful and heavenly.

For Romanians, life was a continuum, and death a mere passage into another world. They lived in the moment, but with a concern for the afterlife. The entire journey is filled with mystery and a desire to be one with nature and at peace with the Universe. Burial rites were and still are important and observed (religious services after 7 days, 40 days, 1 year, etc.).

Literary critic George Călinescu and others[124] consider *Miorița* to be one of the four *defining* myths for the Romanian soul. Another is the folk ballad *Monastirea Argeșului*.

In *Monastirea Argeșului* (or *Meșterul Manole* - Foreman Manole), a team of masons receive orders to build the most splendid monastery under the sun; should they succeed, they will be repaid with exorbitant wealth, should they fail, they will lose their lives. But their work does not last. Everything they build during the day comes crumbling down at night. Eventually, the solution comes to Manole in his dream: he is to bury alive inside the monastery walls the first human being that comes to them in the morning. Alas, that person is his nurturing wife who arrives to bring him food. She initially accepts gladly, as if it were a lovers' game, but soon begins to plead for her life. Despite her pain and her heart-wrenching pleas, he has no choice but to perform this human sacrifice, and thus the walls become glued together and the monastery is completed. When prince Negru Vodă comes to look at it, however, Manole and his team boast that they can build an even more splendid one, and as a result, are condemned to remain stranded on the roof. Manole fashions wooden wings, but crashes and dies (Icarus myth). A well of limpid water marks the spot where he fell.

Romanian folk songs and dances are quite diverse, depending on region and register. They are either very lively and fiery (*sârbe*), raunchy (*cântece lăutărești*, more recently, *manele*), or melancholy and soft (*doine* - songs of love and longing). Romanian folk dances are feisty and typically include a lot of

---

[124] see also Enache, G. in Ziarul Lumina, online edition, "Miturile esențiale ale culturii românești, Miorița și Meșterul Manole,", http://ziarullumina.ro/miturile-esentiale-ale-culturii-romanesti-miorita-si-mesterul-manole-26054.html, 06.04.2016

jumping, swirling (emotional, ritualistic – see *Călușarii*), complex step patterns, and pair dances, but the most typically Romanian dance is the *hora*, a dance in which the participants hold hands to form a full circle, which then unfurls only to come back together again (collectivism, enjoying life together, cosmic elements). The Romanian folk costume is decorated with different colors (mostly red, gold, black, dark red, green), natural and cosmic motifs, and differs from region to region. The entire village comes together for the Church *hram* (or patron holiday), they sit together, laugh, make fun, dance, and there is an abundance of food, wine, and plum brandy. Traditionally, Romanians also had "bride markets", where future weddings were planned, and young men and women from different villages had a chance to meet, flirt, dance, and get to know each other.

Traditional Romanian instruments include the pipe flute, the pan flute (*nai*), the *țambal* (cimbalom, a type of stringed chordophone), *cobză* (a multi-stringed instrument of the lute family), tree leaves, etc.

4.2.2. German vs. Romanian proverbs and sayings

Daniel David (2015) cautions about over-interpreting proverbs, as there are often inconsistent, contradictory, and conflicting proverbs in each culture and it is difficult to know which have had more traction, whether they reflect realities or normative ideals, moral guidance or ironic approaches, are original or imported, etc. This is not an exact science. However, the mere fact that certain proverbs exist and have survived, testifies to the fact that the issues they portray were issues that a critical mass of individuals had to think about, face, and deal with one way or the other.

In a 2005 CURS survey, Romanian respondents declared the following proverbs as most representative for Romania:[125]

1. *Hoțul neprins, negustor cinstit* - 86% (literally, "The unapprehended thief remains an honest merchant", which has to do with corruption)

2. *Face haz de necaz* - 85% (literally, "Makes fun of adversities", which typifies the Romanian way of taking things lightly, not too seriously, poking fun to let off steam, laughing in the face of trouble)

3. *Să moară și capra vecinului* - 83% (literally, "Let the neighbor's goat die, too" - which aptly illustrates the kind of envy a complex of inferiority can breed: in other words, if I cannot succeed, let my neighbor fail as well so that I don't look/feel so bad). In a way, this is the equivalent of the German "Schadenfreude".

Let us nevertheless attempt a comparative analysis of some other common German and Romanian proverbs and sayings along the cultural parameters laid out in Table 6. Germany vs. Romania - Specific overall traits and characteristics of national culture based on the most common models of intercultural communication (page 54, Section 2.2.).

For concision, from the more common (more widely used and best known) proverbs and sayings I have eliminated those which are identical (or extremely similar) in both terminology and meaning and have retained only those which seem to reflect some degree of cultural **difference**. As far as methodology goes, I have used Duden and online sources to determine the more common German proverbs, and have then looked for equivalents, similar but different, or

---

125 David, D., *Psihologia poporului român*, Ed. Polirom, Bucharest, 2015, p. 276 (apud Glăveanu, 2007b)

additional Romanian proverbs and sayings on that particular topic. For instance, "*Den Freund erkennt man in der Not*" = "*Prietenul la nevoie se cunoaşte*" (A friend in need is a friend indeed) are identical and have therefore been left out.

TIME - GERMANY	Observations
"*Langsam aber sicher*" = Slow but secure/safe	Diligent, slow process is a positive thing, it helps avoid future problems
"*Morgenstund' hat Gold im Mund*" = The early bird catches the worm (lit., the early hour has gold in its mouth)	Disciplined daily routine. Probably the best-known German proverb[126].
"*Rom wurde nicht an einem Tag erbaut*" = Rome was not built in a day	Good results take time

TIME - ROMANIA	Observations
"*Ho, că doar nu dau/vin turcii!*" = (lit.) (Stop/no need to hurry) the Turks aren't coming!	Used to <u>moderate unnecessarily hasty behavior</u>. Historical reference to frequent Turkish/Tatar invasions in the Middle Ages.

---

[126]Duden, *Sprichwörter und Redewendungen aus aller Welt*, Dudenverlag, Berlin, 2014, p. 62

TIME - ROMANIA	Observations
"Graba strică treaba" = Hurriedness/hastiness ruins the work	<u>Indirect</u> suggestion that slower, more careful consideration would be better
"Cine se scoală de dimineață, departe ajunge" = The early bird catches the worm (lit., who gets up early in the morning, will go a long way)	Against laziness, in favor of industriousness (seems to refer to merchants, travelers, getting things done). Very similar to German.
"A plecat cu graba și s-a întâlnit cu zăbava" = He was full of impetus at first, but lost it along the way, didn't get much done after all (lit., he left in a hurry and met with dalliance along the way)	<u>Inconstancy</u>; good start but suboptimal end result.

Table 10. German and Romanian proverbs and sayings about time

COMMUNICATION AND EMOTION - GERMANY	Observations
"Hochmut kommt vor dem Fall" = Pride goes before a fall	Hubris is a sin and can make one careless
"Hunde, die bellen, beißen nicht" = A barking dog never bites	Barking often means a threat to stay away, at a safe distance; dogs cannot bite while they are barking.
"Die Sprache ist der Spiegel der Gedanken" = Your speech reflects your thoughts (lit., language is the mirror of thoughts)	One speaks from what one believes, speech reflects inner thought. Compare with the Romanian version, where the eyes are the mirror of the soul = indirect, non-verbal clues are important!
"Wenn du in Rom bist, handele wie ein Römer" = When in Rome, do as Romans do	Respect for local customs; adapt, try not to challenge them.

COMMUNICATION AND EMOTION - ROMANIA	Observations
"Vorba dulce mult aduce" = Sweet talk goes a long way (lit., sweet words bring you a lot of good)	<u>How</u> one talks is also important, tactful, flattering.

COMMUNICATION AND EMOTION - ROMANIA	Observations
"Câinele care latră nu mușcă" = A barking dog never bites	In Romanian, this also has the nuance that people <u>who can let off steam (bark) are no longer dangerous</u> (they will speak but not act).
"Ce-i în gușă, și-n căpușă" = What is in their mouth (lit., throat), is what is in their head	As an excuse, for someone who is too direct, tactless - at least you know they say exactly what they think/feel.
"Ochii sunt oglinda sufletului" = One's eyes reflect (lit., are the mirror of) one's soul	In communication, eye contact can reveal a lot (<u>non-verbal</u>)
"De vorbă bună nu te doare gura" = (lit.) Your mouth won't hurt if you say a kind word	You can always speak kindly to another person, it won't cost you anything.
"Degeaba ai trăit, dacă pe nimeni n-ai iubit" = (lit.) You have lived in vain if you haven't loved anybody	<u>Love</u> (both sensuous and brotherly) is the spice of life, it gives meaning to life.
"Bate șaua ca să priceapă iapa" = (lit.) Hit the saddle, so that the mare understands	Communicate unpleasant truths <u>indirectly.</u>

COMMUNICATION AND EMOTION - ROMANIA	Observations
"Lauda de sine nu miroase-a bine" = (lit.) Self-praise smells bad	One should not act too arrogant, hubris stinks, is seen as bad - similar to the German version. Modesty is preferred.
"Bucuria mare e cea mai scurtă" = (lit.) The biggest joy is the most short-lived	(Positive) <u>emotions are usually intense</u>, <u>but short-lived.</u>
"Greşeala recunoscută e pe jumătate iertată" = (lit.) A mistake already admitted is half forgiven	Open communication of mistakes leads to forgiveness. <u>Understanding.</u>
"Dacă-ţi place să fii musafir, să-ţi placă şi gazdă să fii" = (lit.) If you enjoy being a guest, you should also enjoy being a host	<u>Hospitality</u> (but combined with another proverb, "Don't make your doors bigger than your house", it shows not everyone is always welcome.)
"Fie pâinea cât de rea, tot mai bună-n ţara ta" = (lit.) No matter how bad the bread is, at home in your country it tastes better	<u>Romanian attachment to the</u> <u>motherland, love for home.</u>

Table 11. German and Romanian proverbs and sayings about communication and emotion

STRUCTURE AND ACTION - GERMANY	Observations
"*Besser den Spatz in der Hand als die Taube auf dem Dach*" = A bird in the hand is worth two in the bush (lit., better the sparrow in the hand, als the dove on the roof)	<u>Risk-aversity, restrained</u> culture, what's certain is certain.
"*Müßiggang ist aller Laster Anfang*" = Idleness is the root of all evil	Christian work ethic.
"*Eine Schwalbe macht noch keinen Sommer*" = = One swallow does not a summer make	A good start is not enough, does not mean the work is already done.
"*Not macht erfinderisch*" = Necessity is the mother of invention	Tough circumstances make creativity necessary.
"*Ein guter Name ist besser als Geld*" = A good name is better than riches	Good reputation, good character is worth its weight in gold.
"*Ende gut, alles gut*" = All's well that ends well "*Das Ende krönt das Werk*" = The end crowns the work	What really matters in the end, is success; result-oriented culture. The good end result is its own prize.
"*Viele Köche verderben den Brei*" = Too many cooks spoil the broth	Too many leaders in charge, bad organization can run everything into the ground.
"*Wie der Herr, so's Gescherr*" =	One's habits and negligence are easily seen in one's

STRUCTURE AND ACTION - GERMANY	Observations
Like master, like man (lit. like master, so his tools)	home/possessions, etc. Need for order. Example comes from the top. (Top-down approach).
"Der Mensch denkt, Gott lenkt" = Man proposes, God disposes	Biblical. One can make plans, but one needs the assistance of higher forces to have them come true.
"Geist ist gut, aber Verstand besser" = (lit.) Spirit is good, but reason is better	<u>Rationality, objectivity</u> is preferred to wit.

STRUCTURE AND ACTION - ROMANIA	Observations
"Nu da vrabia din mână pe cioara de pe gard" = A bird in the hand is worth two in the bush (lit., do not give the sparrow in your hand for the crow on the fence)	<u>Risk-averse, restrained culture</u>. In Romanian, there is the additional nuance that <u>what seems tempting might not even be so great</u> (it is a crow, not a dove).
"Leneșul mai mult aleargă (și zgârcitul mai mult păgubește)" = Idleness leads to more effort (and avarice to more waste) (lit., the lazy person ends up running more, and the avaricious ends up with bigger losses)	Practical advice against laziness and avarice. What seems comfortable at the current moment carries a heavier price down the road. Smart people aren't cheap.
"Cu o floare nu se face primăvară" = = (lit.) One flower does not a spring make	A good start is not enough, does not mean the work is already done. <u>Climate differences</u>: spring

STRUCTURE AND ACTION - ROMANIA	Observations
	instead of summer as propitious (good weather starts sooner).
"Nevoia te învață" = Necessity is the mother of invention, but also: *"Nevoia te duce și pe unde nu ți-e voia"* = (lit.) Need will take you where you do not want to go	Tough circumstances make creativity necessary. In combination with the second proverb, it shows that necessity can also lead to <u>compromise</u>, not only invention (need also has <u>negative aspects</u>).
"Meseria e brățară de aur" = A good profession is worth a fortune (lit. a good craft is a golden bracelet)	A good profession/skill/ craft is worth a lot in the world.
"Domnia și prostia se plătesc" = Pretentiousness and stupidity carry a heavy price	Arrogant laziness and stupidity are bad things.
"Copilul cu prea multe moaște rămâne cu buricul netăiat" = (lit.) The child with too many midwives will remain with his umbilicus uncut)	Do not put too many people in charge, they can ruin the result, because everybody counts on somebody else to take the necessary action.
"Cum e turcul, și pistolul" = Like master, like man (lit. like the Turk, so his pistol)	One's habits (order or negligence) are easily seen in one's home/possessions, etc. Like the person, so his actions.

STRUCTURE AND ACTION - ROMANIA	Observations
"Fuga-i rușinoasă, dar e sănătoasă" = (lit.) Running away may be shameful, but it is healthy	Fleeing can get you out of danger, although it damages your reputation.
"După faptă, și răsplată" = The consequence matches the deed	Need for justice. Consequences necessarily derive from the deed, and reward/retribution should match it.
"Cine fură azi un ou, mâine va fura un bou" = He who takes a pin may take a better thing (lit., who steals an egg today, will steal an ox tomorrow)	Realistic and cynical. Once a thief, always a thief. Stop bad habits while they are still small.
"Unde-i lege, nu-i tocmeală" = (lit.) Where there is law, there is no bargaining	<u>Universalism (declared, normative)</u>. Admiration for strong government, no loopholes, no bargaining.
"Încercarea moarte n-are" = it's always worth a try, it can't hurt to try	<u>Particularism</u>. Try, perhaps it will work.
"La un car de minte, e bine să fie și un dram de noroc" = (lit.) For a cart of good sense, it helps if there is also a pinch of good luck	<u>Realism, pragmatism</u>: reason alone does not suffice, individual ability is not enough, one needs the right opportunity and luck.

STRUCTURE AND ACTION - ROMANIA	Observations
"Cine n-a dormit pe piatră între străini, nu știe prețul rogojinii de-acasă" = (lit.) Who has not slept on slabs of stone among foreigners does not know the value of the bast mat from home	Perception is relative. Expatriates often appreciate their home country more, because they have experienced difficulties abroad. Strong family and national ties.
"Omul sfințește locul" = (lit.) Places are made holy by men	A place is as good as the people inhabiting it. Good men make even derelict places bloom.
"Banul e ochiul dracului" = (lit.) Money is the evil eye, the temptation	Against materialism.
"Brânză bună în burduf de câine" = (lit.) Good cheese, in dog bellows	Good intentions/talent are not enough if the environment is not conducive, the methods are wrong, or some other virtue is missing.
"Cine nu deschide ochii, deschide punga" = If you don't pay attention, you will have to open your purse	In the world, one had better not be naive, watch out. <u>Realism</u>.
"Ca vodă prin lobodă" = swagger along, carefree and careless (lit., as the Ruler/Prince through the high grass)	<u>Carelessness</u>, lack of consideration for detail

Table 12. German and Romanian proverbs and sayings about structure and action

HUMAN RELATIONSHIPS AND COMPETITIVENESS - GERMANY	Observations
"Wenn man unter Wölfe ist, muss man mit ihnen heulen" = Who keeps company with wolves will (lit. must) learn to howl	Entourage is influence. One must not stand out, one follows the same moral behavior
"So viele Köpfe, so viele Sinne" = So many men, so many minds (lit. so many heads, so many senses)	People have different ideas, truth can be relative.
"Den letzten beißen die Hunde" = The devil will take the hindmost	The last suffers the most, (winner takes all, milder in German than English).

HUMAN RELATIONSHIPS AND COMPETITIVENESS - ROMANIA	Observations
"Câte capete, atâtea păreri" = (lit.) So many heads, so many opinions, but also *"Câte bordeie, atâtea obicee"* = (lit.) So many huts, so many traditions	First version identical with German, second adds an <u>awareness of cultural differences</u>, <u>tolerance</u>
"Urma scapă turma" = The last one saves the herd	Different nuance for the last - he suffers but saves the herd.
"Nu este om fără cusur" = Nobody is perfect	<u>Leniency</u>, <u>tolerance of human weakness.</u>

HUMAN RELATIONSHIPS AND COMPETITIVENESS - ROMANIA	Observations
"Prea multă minte strică, prea puțină nu e bună de nimică" = (lit.) Too much reason hurts, too little is good for nothing	<u>Dislike</u> of <u>sophisticated intellectuals</u> and <u>excessive rationality</u> prefer the middle way.
"Omul vrednic se face luntre și punte și iese la mal" = A worthy man will do everything in his power to succeed (lit., a worthy man will turn himself into a boat and a bridge and will manage to come ashore)	Praise for <u>resourcefulness</u> in finding solutions (the imagery is that of <u>survival</u>, risk of drowning otherwise). <u>Individualism,</u> initiative.
"Frate-frate, dar brânza-i pe bani" = (lit.) We may be brothers, but the cheese costs money	<u>Realism</u>. Profiteering is not appreciated. Using informal connections to solve problems is widespread in Romania, but there should be a fair exchange of favors; fair business practices should be observed; <u>negative light on stinginess</u>. One should help one's <u>family</u> out.
"Pe cine nu lași să moară, nu te lasă să trăiești" = Who you do not leave to die, won't allow you to live	Again, <u>realism</u> and <u>cynicism</u> from experience.

HUMAN RELATIONSHIPS AND COMPETITIVENESS - ROMANIA	Observations
"Nu-ți cumpăra casă, cumpără-ți un vecin" = (lit.) Do not buy a house, buy a neighbor	People are at least as important as objects. Getting along is important.
"Rufele murdare se spală în familie" = Dirty linen should be washed in the family	<u>Collectivism. Family ties. Saving face</u>.
"La plăcinte înainte, la război înapoi" = (lit.) First when it comes to pie, last when it comes to fighting a war	About someone who wants only the easy part, the benefits, and is not loyal in times of trouble. <u>A free rider in a collectivist society</u>.

Table 13. **German and Romanian proverbs and sayings about human relationships and competitiveness**

POWER - GERMANY	Observations
"Wissen ist Macht" = Knowledge (information) is power	Power lies in knowledge, know-how, information (<u>individualism</u>)
"Wer nicht wagt, der nicht gewinnt" = No risk, no gain	Winning means <u>taking chances, individually.</u>

POWER - ROMANIA	Observations
"Unde-s doi, puterea crește" = Two are better than one (lit., where there are two, power increases)	Power lies in numbers (<u>collectivism</u>).
"Fă-te frate și cu dracul până treci puntea" = (lit.) Befriend (become the brother of) even the devil until you have crossed the bridge	Power and survival lie in making <u>compromises</u>, having strong <u>allies</u>, being <u>on good terms with powerful people</u>
"La omul sărac, nici boii nu-i trag" = (lit.) For the impoverished, even the oxen won't pull	<u>Poor people</u> have no power and no chance to prosper, everything is against them.
"Ban la ban trage" = (lit.) Money is attracted to money	It is easier for the rich to get richer (than for the poor).
"Peștele de la cap se împute" = (lit.) The fish starts to deteriorate (decay, degenerate and stink) from its head	<u>Leaders are to blame</u>, theirs is the responsibility; if the leader is corrupt, the whole country corrupt.

POWER - ROMANIA	Observations
"Când pisica nu-i acasă, șoarecii joacă pe masă" = when the cat is not at home, the mice dance on the table	<u>Strong leadership is important; when the leader is absent, everyone vies for his position, structures fall apart.</u>
"Cine-mparte, parte-și face" = the person in charge of distributing the goodies, will take the lion's share	<u>Power brings with it privilege.</u>

Table 14. German and Romanian proverbs and sayings about power

ENVIRONMENT - GERMANY	Observations
"Hilf dir selbst, dann hilft dir Gott" = God helps those who help themselves	Private initiative, <u>individualism</u>
"Wer nicht wagt, der nicht gewinnt" = No risk, no gain	Winning means <u>taking chances, individually.</u>
"Man soll den Tag nicht vor dem Abend loben" = Don't count your chickens before they are hatched (lit., do not praise the day before it becomes evening)	Results can only be evaluated once work is finished. They are not guaranteed, must pay attention until the end (<u>internal locus of control</u>)

ENVIRONMENT - ROMANIA	Observations
"Dumnezeu cu mila" = At God's mercy, *"Cum o da Dumnezeu"* =	<u>Fatalism, more passive,</u> contemplative, trusting Providence

As God wills it (lit., as God shall give)	
"*A se duce pe apa Sâmbetei*" = To go down the drain (lit., to go down the waters of the Saturday river)	Missed opportunity, waste, degradation
"*N-aduce anul ce aduce ceasul*" = Life is full of unexpected things (lit., a whole year might not bring what one hour brings)	We cannot control chance and hazard (<u>external locus of control</u>)
"*Ziua bună se cunoaște de dimineață*" = (lit.) One can recognize a good day based on how the morning is	A good start of the day means we will have a good day overall (<u>opposite of similar German saying!</u>).
"*Norocu-i după cum și-l face omul*" = Luck is as one makes it (we make our own luck)	Personal initiative, not mere reliance on luck.
"*Boală lungă, moarte sigură*" = (lit.) Lingering disease means certain death	<u>Pessimism</u>, realism, fatalism.
"*Năravul din fire, n-are lecuire*" = (lit.) The vice you were born with cannot be cured	Heredity, <u>skepticism</u>.

Table 15. German and Romanian proverbs and sayings about control of the environment

4.3. Ready for conversation? German vs. Romanian idiomatic expressions and set phrases

4.3.1. German vs. Romanian idiomatic expressions

It is not the purpose of this book to present an exhaustive hermeneutic analysis or comparison of the two languages; that would be a daunting task in its own right, for which we do not possess the right instruments. Let us only very briefly discuss some of the most salient aspects of speech communication based on a few examples of idiomatic expressions along the lines of the cultural categories laid out in chapter 2.2, as well as a shortlist of set phrases, representative of the two cultures.

The focus here is on Romanian, of which I am a native speaker.

GERMAN	ROMANIAN	Notes
TIME		
Gleich (immediately, but not as prompt) *sofort!* (very demanding, very prompt)	*imediat...* (immediately = I'll get to you as soon as I finish all the other things I'm doing (could be hours)	Romanian time is not as linear and structured, it is more flexible and uncertain.
	lung ca o zi de post (long as a fasting day)	Impatience, short-term orientation.
Wie die Zeit vergeht (how time goes away)	*Ce zboară timpul!* (how time flies)	Flying is faster than going (shorter-term orientation).
	cât ai zice pește! (as quickly as you can say 'fish' = very rapidly)	Plastic Romanian expression for quickness.

GERMAN	ROMANIAN	Notes
TIME		
	la Paştele cailor (lit., at the horses' Easter = never)	Plastic Romanian expression for never.

GERMAN	ROMANIAN	Notes
SPACE		
Sehr weit (very far) *Noch ein gutes Stück* (still a fair distance away)	*la mama dracului* (at the mother of the devil), *la dracu in praznic* (at the devil's feast)	Germany: either precise or understated, Romania: hyperbole, graphic language.
	cu fundul în două luntri (with one's bottom in two boats)	Undecided (fluid and intersecting spheres).
Riesengroß, riesig (huge, enormous)	*cât casa*, lately *cât China* (as big as a house, as big as China)	German: clear and standard. Romanian tends to overstate, rhetorical tricks.
sich verschanzen (to entrench oneself), *sich abschotten* (to encapsulate oneself)	*a se baricada* (to barricade oneself), no Romanian equivalent for "*abschotten*"	German version creates the impression of much deeper closure.
dicht machen (to close shop, lit., to make something tight, airproof)	*a trage obloanele/cortina* (to close a project, an undertaking)	Again, the German version suggests more tightness.
auf eigene Kosten/Rechnung/Gefahr (on one's own expense /account /peril)	*pe propria piele* (on one's own skin)	Money vs. own body = thing- vs. person-orientation.

GERMAN	ROMANIAN	Notes
COMMUNICATION AND EMOTION		
Sehnsucht (longing yearning, nostalgia), *Wehmut* (woefulness, melancholy)	*dor* (longing, yearning, nostalgia, wistfulness, almost pain), *a duce dorul cuiva* (lit., to carry a longing for someone = to miss someone badly)	German has several different concepts, more specific. Romanian has a 'one-fits-all', intense and untranslatable notion, used for people, country, places, times, etc.
	vai și amar! (with hand gesture; it means, literally, "ouch and bitterness")	A typically Romanian expression of weary dislike ("*lehamite*").
	a vorbi la pereți (to talk to the walls), *a-și bate gura de pomană* (to beat one's mouth in vain, to talk to the wind)	Romanians like feedback, encountering rigidity is like talking to the walls.
	a se înțelege ca mutul cu surdul (lit., to understand each other like the mute and the deaf), *de parcă vorbesc cu turcii* (as if talking to the Turks)	Not being able to understand each other. Historical reference to the Turks (understanding is impossible).
Um den heißen Brei herum reden (to talk around the hot pulp)	*a bate câmpii* (to beat around the bush - lit., to beat the fields)	German version seems to indicate this is done to avoid a hot topic; Romanian: person talks beside the point and loses track.
	a nu-și mai încăpea în piele de bucurie/de mândrie (to not fit into one's skin for joy/pride)	Extreme <u>emotionality</u>, which comes from within but flows over into the public space.
Fetzen fliegen (rags are flying - angry, heated argument)	*a-i sări țandăra* (one's splinter/fuse explodes - choleric behavior)	German imagery is that of old rags flying about.

GERMAN	ROMANIAN	Notes
COMMUNICATION AND EMOTION		
		Romanian: head explodes (more intense).
	a se supăra ca prostul pe sat (lit., to get upset like the village idiot at the village, without reason)	Romanian: it is stupid to end relationships/friendships for a trifle.
Ein Sturm im Wasserglas (a storm in a teacup/in a glass of water)	*a face din țânțar armăsar* (lit., to turn a mosquito into a stallion/steed)	The German version has to do with inanimate natural elements. The Romanian version is more ludicrous.
	a scoate din pepeni (lit., to bring someone out of their melons = to irritate them until they lose control)	Plastic Romanian expression about getting irked.
	a sta cu limba în gură (lit., to sit with one's tongue in one's mouth, not express an opinion, not greet)	Lack of opinion or rhetorical skill is seen as a sign of dull personality, asocial behavior, limited wit.
	a da sfoară în țară (lit., to send cable across the country)	To notify everyone, let everyone know.
	a duce pe cineva cu vorba/cu zăhărelul/cu preșul (lit. to lead someone on with words/sugar/with the carpet, to string along)	Saying what one wants to hear, flattering and lying.
	a face capul calendar (to fill someone's head with too many unnecessary details)	Pragmatism, impatience. Too many details are boring.
Schwamm drüber! (No hard feelings -	*a o lăsa moartă* (lit., to leave it for dead = drop a contentious topic)	German: cleaning imagery.

GERMAN	ROMANIAN	Notes
COMMUNICATION AND EMOTION		
lit., wipe over with a sponge)		Romanian: diplomacy, do not insist on a hot topic, let it die quietly.
	a se simți cu musca pe căciulă (lit., to feel the fly on one's hat = feel guilty)	Plastic Romanian expression about guilt.
	a cădea în butoiul cu melancolie (lit., to fall in the melancholy barrel = to become quiet, nostalgic)	Too quiet = sad, melancholy.
	la inimă este-un leac/cetera și omul drag (lit., there is one cure for the heart: the lute and the lover)	Romanian emotionality, love, singing, playing music.

GERMAN	ROMANIAN	Notes
STRUCTURE AND ACTION		
	țara lui Papură-Vodă (a place where there is no consideration for rules, everyone does what they want, no accountability)	Typical Romanian complaint about the way their country is run, or the way people behave. <u>Bad governance</u>.
der Teufel liegt im Detail (the devil is in the details" = details must be taken into consideration	*taie și fluieră* (lit., chops and whistles = cuts first, measures later)	RO: unbothered, carefree action, <u>without much concern for consequences</u>
	a se afla în treabă, a-și face de lucru (lit., to find oneself in the process, to pretend	Romanian expression for someone who is not rigourous in their work

GERMAN	ROMANIAN	Notes
STRUCTURE AND ACTION		
	one is working, to waste time)	or is not competent in that field.
Immer mit der Ruhe. (Hold your horses! Do not get all worked up)	*stai calm / şezi blând* (mostly in Transylvania) (stay calm, sit softly) *nu te agita* (stop stirring), *nu-ţi lua viteză* (do not pick up speed), *ce te oftici aşa?!* (why do you get so riled up?!)	German version indicates <u>patience</u> and a desire to do away with the initial hot emotional state. Romanian versions are affirmative and peaceful only in certain regions, the others are mocking, attempting to stop inner turmoil, speed of speech associated with anger.
Sachlichkeit (lit., thingliness = objectivity, facts)	*obiectivitate*	A typical German trait and a must in communication, work, action.
überlegen, nachdenken (to think something over, to reflect, to ponder, to consider). *Interestingly enough, as an adjective, "überlegen" means superior!*	*a se (mai) gândi* (to think (some more)	The Romanian version is less precise. ("to reflect", "to meditate", "to take into consideration" also exist, but they are not common in everyday speech.) German: indicates <u>long and thorough thinking</u>, considering and reconsidering.
	mai catolic decât Papa (more Catholic than the Pope = dogmatic, a stickler, putting external rules above people)	Dogmatism is considered a negative thing in Romania.

GERMAN	ROMANIAN	Notes
STRUCTURE AND ACTION		
hinschmeißen (to pack in, to chuck, quit) - more active and direct, to throw in the towel	*a lăsa baltă* (lit. to leave it a puddle = to drop it, to give up, quit smth.)	Romanian expression suggests more carelessness, indifference, not carrying things through, the German version is more pro-active.
Nagel auf dem Kopf treffen (to hit the nail on the head = to find the perfect explanation)	*unde dai și unde crapă* (lit., where you hit, and where it cracks = misunderstanding or hazard)	German: to be right on target. Romanian: hazard is sometimes stronger than precision, communication may be misunderstood.
Die Wand hochgehen (go ballistic, go berserk, climb up the wall)	*a se sui pe pereți* (go up the wall), but also *a-și lua câmpii* (actually get so mad as to want to drop everything and go away)	Romanian: when it's really bad, one only wants to get away from it all: "take to one's fields"
sich mit etwas auseinandersetzen (to debate something, to deal with something - the focus is on sparring, contending, fighting, tackling)		The German noun *Auseinandersetzung* means argument, dispute, conflict, contention, but also settlement. The nuance of the verb is that of a face-off with the issue at hand, literally taking the issue apart; debate and eventually settlement by way of incisive analysis.
Sparmaßnahmen (austerity measures,	*a se întinde cât îi e plapuma* (lit., to stretch only as far as	German terms are almost untranslatable in

GERMAN	ROMANIAN	Notes
STRUCTURE AND ACTION		
savings), *Altersvorsorge* (provisions for retirement, pension plans) = a focus on foreseeing risks and acting to counter them	the covers allow = to exhibit restraint, limit one's needs to fit the constraints)	Romanian and indicate <u>long-term orientation,</u> <u>concern with material</u> <u>things</u>, desire to <u>plan and</u> <u>control</u> the future. Romanian has the nuance of someone who <u>adapts</u>, without pro-actively doing anything to avoid future discomfort.
Unterlagen (documents, documentation, paperwork that lays the foundation for a job interview /work / etc.), *Zeugnis* (certificate, proof, credential)	*documentație* / no single word in Romanian for *Zeugnisse*; *Bewerbungsmappe* not common. *Hârțogărie* (red tape, excessive paperwork)	Typically German term. Extensive and indispensable documentation. <u>Excessive paperwork is</u> <u>seen as negative in</u> <u>Romania.</u>
Fach/Sachgebiet, fachlich, (derived from compartment: subject/trade - specialist/profession al)	*(de) specialitate* (derived from special)	The German term for specialist trade - indicates <u>compartmentalization</u>
Zielstrebig, Zielstrebigkeit (determined, single-mindedness)		No direct Romanian equivalent ("ambitious, zealous"). <u>Linearity and</u> <u>target orientation.</u>
"lassen wir die Kirche im Dorf" (let us not get carried	*a se da de ceasul morții* (lit., to hit against the hour of death = desperately try to	Romanian version indicates stressful, last-

GERMAN	ROMANIAN	Notes
STRUCTURE AND ACTION		
away – lit., let us leave the church in the village)	solve a problem under extreme time pressure and stress)	minute action. (<u>Type A management style</u>).
	a fi un pierde-vară (lit., to be a summer-waster = to be lazy, unreliable), *a freca menta* (lit., to rub the peppermint = to waste time, do nothing)	Someone who has <u>no real plan/goal/structure;</u> often used for public servants
	a munci până îți sar capacele (lit., to work until your lid pops = to work very hard)	More recent Romanian expression (for demanding corporate job or physical work)
	a-i merge mintea brici (lit., somebody's mind is sharp as a razor = to be very intelligent, creative, fast)	<u>Creativity, spontaneity, pragmatism</u>
	a îngrășa porcul în Ajun (lit., to fatten the pig on Christmas Eve = to take late and superficial action)	<u>Quick, superficial solutions.</u>
	mi se rupe/mi se fâlfâie (I don't give a rat's ass/ I don't give a flying freak), *miserupist* (such a person)	<u>Laxity about rules, duties, expectations</u>
	a sta strâmb și a judeca drept (lit., to stand askance and to judge correctly = think things over, acknowledge truth)	Look at things from the right angle and admit the reality
	a fi prins cu mâța în sac (lit., get caught with the cat in the bag = caught telling lies)	Plastic expression about lying (it is akin to stealing)

GERMAN	ROMANIAN	Notes
STRUCTURE AND ACTION		
	mintea românului cea de pe urmă (lit., the Romanian's last afterthought, last sense)	Negative meaning: the Romanian does <u>not think carefully enough</u> in advance, only in hindsight does he come to his senses and see a more rational way.

GERMAN	ROMANIAN	Notes
HUMAN RELATIONSHIPS AND COMPETITIVENESS		
	ca lumea (lit., like the world = great, nice, good quality, in line with the world	This untranslatable Romanian term indicates <u>gregariousness</u>. Do as the world does. What everyone has/does is/must be valuable.
	cumsecade (nice, decent, as is appropriate)	RO: <u>collectivism</u>, moral convention.
	a nu fi uşă de biserică (lit., he is not a church door, he is not exactly a saint, but he is still secretly admired)	Tolerance for human weakness, plastic language. Understatement.
	neobrăzat, obraznic, cu obraz gros (lit., cheekless = cheeky, brazen)	Shows concern with "face", keeping and saving face.
	a lăsa în plata Domnului (stop bothering with a stubborn person, let them do as they please, leave them to God's judgment)	Drop it, let them do as they please. <u>Flexibility, tolerance, forgiveness.</u>

GERMAN	ROMANIAN	Notes
	a fi vioara întâi (to be first violin = to be the star, the leader) vs. *a fi a cincea roată la căruță* (to be the fifth wheel = to be one too many, to not fit in).	Romanian <u>competitiveness</u>
Existenzangst haben, unter Existenzangst leiden (to Suffer from existential fear, fear of losing one's livelihood)	*se împute treaba* (lit., the situation is beginning to stink = things are getting worse)	The German version is a composite noun and untranslatable into Romanian. It is very serious and dire.
getrennt zahlen (to pay separately - this has been translated into Romanian either as to pay separately, or to pay German-style)	*a face cinste* (lit., to do someone the honesty /the honor = to pay for their drinks/food/tickets when going out	Romanian versions show limited concern with money among friends, <u>person-orientation</u>, (friends alternatively pay for each other). German version indicates a <u>separation of spheres, precision</u>.
	a face casă bună cu cineva (lit., to make a good house with someone = to get along)	Liking each other, living peacefully is appreciated in Romania.
	șmecher vs. *fraier* (smart alec, dishonest person who cuts corners and always ends up on his feet vs."loser", honest person)	This shows that honesty in Romania is still seen as not paying off; street-smart stands a better chance. <u>Disregard for</u>

HUMAN RELATIONSHIPS AND COMPETITIVENESS

GERMAN	ROMANIAN	Notes
		HUMAN RELATIONSHIPS AND COMPETITIVENESS
		rules, preference for spontaneous solutions.
Sich durchwursteln (muddle through, get by without real effort or investment)	*descurcăreț* (resourceful, someone who can always manage to find a way and disembroil himself from problems or obstacles)	For Romanians, this is a positive notion, for the Germans a negative one.
	a fi dat dracului, a fi uns cu toate alifiile (lit., to be given to the devil, to be oiled with all potions = to be resourceful in a smart but rather dishonest way)	See above. Secret admiration for people who are intimate with the "tricks of the devil".
	a fi pâinea lui Dumnezeu (lit. to be as good as God's bread, as good as Holy Communion = to be extremely kind)	Kindness and generosity. (association with godliness).
	a-și vedea lungul nasului (lit., to see the length of one's nose = to know one's place, to not overestimate one's worth)	People (in inferior positions) are supposed to know their limits and their place. Collectivism and ascription.
Streber (striver, eager beaver = negative)	*tocilar* (someone who crams and learns by heart, also negative)	German: strives too hard to get ahead; Romanian: learns by heart, hits the same spot until it becomes blunt.
	aceeași Mărie cu altă pălărie (lit., the same Mary with a different hat = same old, same old)	Romanian skepticism, everything is the way it always was, only appearances change.

GERMAN	ROMANIAN	Notes
HUMAN RELATIONSHIPS AND COMPETITIVENESS		
	a-și vedea numai interesul lui (to see only one's own interest)	In Romania, this is a negative thing (=selfishness, asocial behavior)
	a fi zgârie-brânză (lit., to scratch the cheese, to be extremely stingy)	Romanian: stinginess is very negative.

GERMAN	ROMANIAN	Notes
POWER		
	a avea pâinea și cuțitul în mână (lit., to have the bread and the knife in the hand = to have power and opportunity), *a tăia și a spânzura* (lit., to cut and hang = to be undemocratic, brutal, arbitrary)	Very vivid Romanian expressions about <u>exercising power despotically</u>. The first one is used when people waste opportunities despite having had ideal conditions.
	a se pune bine cu cineva (to flatter someone to get under their skin, to be on good terms with them)	RO: <u>concerning powerful and influential people.</u>
	a ține de scaun (to hold on to one's chair)	RO: stubborn and greedy <u>determination not to leave a position of power</u>

GERMAN	ROMANIAN	Notes
ENVIRONMENT		
Hut brennt (we are in serious trouble, lit., our hat is burning)	*am dat de dracu* (we have come across the devil), *ne-am dat foc la casă* (we've set fire to our own house)	RO: "we have come across the devil" = <u>external forces</u> at play; second version more internal control.
Alles im Grunen Bereich (everything is ok), traffic light and computer analogy	*suntem în grafic* (we are on schedule)	This recent Romanian idiom shows <u>more structured time and internal locus of control</u>
	cine știe ce-o mai fi până atunci (who knows what will happen until then)	Romanian: <u>external locus of control</u>, life is controlled by hazard/Providence.

Table 16. A brief comparative analysis of common idiomatic expressions in German and Romanian

4.3.2. German vs. Romanian set phrases, wishes, small talk

Below is a brief outline of some of the most commonly used standard expressions and set formulas in both languages:

Situation	GERMAN	ROMANIAN	Notes
Calling after an unknown person in the street	*"Hallo!"* (Hello, Hey!)	*"Nu vă supărați..."* (Do not get upset...) – used to introduce a request *"Domnule/Doamnă/Băiete / Domnișoară!"* (Mister/Madam/Lady/Boy/ Miss!)	Calling "Alo!" after someone is considered quite abrupt and rude in Romania.
Asking for directions	*"Entschuldigung..."* / *"Entschuldigen Sie..."* (Apologies / Excuse me)	*"Nu vă supărați... "* / *"Fiți amabil(ă) /"Mă scuzați..."* (Do not get upset.... / Would you be so kind... / Excuse me...)	The Romanian phrase indicates more deference. Generally, Germans only say "Entschuldigung" when there is something to excuse.
Greeting people	*"Hallo/Guten Morgen/ Tag/*	*"Bună (dimineața/ziua/seara)"*	Bavarian greetings often refer to God (may God greet

Situation	GERMAN	ROMANIAN	Notes
	Abend/ Grüß Gott (BY)"	(Good morning/day/evening), *"Să trăiți!"* (lit., May you live! = very formal, respectful, borrowed from the military - for older superiors)	you, may God lead you).
Asking how they are	*"Wie geht's?"* (How are you, how is it going) *"Alles gut?"* (everything well?) *"Gut, danke"* / *"es geht"*... *"und selber? / und Ihnen?"* (well, thank you/so and so/ and yourself?) = standard answer	*"Ce mai faci / Ce mai faceți?"* (How are you doing - lit., so what else have you been doing?) *"Bine, mulțumesc, /Așa și așa / nu prea grozav dumneavoastră / tu?"* (well /not so great, thank you, and yourself?) = the short standard answer	In Germany, the answer is usually another set phrase. In Romania, people go into more personal detail, and can actually start telling what they have been doing, whether they are happy/sad/tired/ill, what the children are doing, etc.
The decision to	*"Glückwunsch/ Gratulation"*	*"Felicitări!"* (Congratulations!) *"Mă*	In Romania, these often include

Situation	GERMAN	ROMANIAN	Notes
get married, or pregnancy	(Congratulations), *"Ich freue mich für euch"* (I am happy for you"	*bucur pentru voi!"* (I am happy for you!) *"Să fie într-un ceas bun!"* (Let it happen in a blessed hour!) *"Naștere ușoară!"* (Easy labor/childbirth!)	some type of body language and contact: hugs, kisses, handshakes.
Marriage	*"Herzlichen Glückwunsch!"* / *"Gratulation!"* (Congratulations!)	*"Casă de piatră!"* (May you have a house of stone!)	In Romanian, this standard phrase must always be said to the married couple (biblical reference - a house only lasts if built on stone).
Birth of a child, baptism, Christening	*"Glückwunsch zum Baby"* (Congratulation for your baby) *"Glückwunsch/Alles Gute",* (Congratulations and all the best!) = less common for Christening	*"Felicitări! Să vă trăiască!"* (Congratulations! Long may he/she live!) *"Să vă bucurați de el!"* (May you enjoy the child!) *"Să vă aducă numai bucurii!"* (May the child bring you nothing but joy!)	RO: Reflects old traditions, when many young children died before the age of 5. Showing enthusiasm about other people's children is an

Situation	GERMAN	ROMANIAN	Notes
			important social skill.
Birthday, anniversary	*"Herzlichen Glückwunsch (zum Geburtstag)!"* (Happy Birthday) *"Alles Gute!"* (All the best!) *"Hoch soll er leben!"/"Dreimal hoch!"* (Three cheers, lit., high may he live!)	*"La mulți ani!"* (Many more years!) *"Mulți înainte!"* (Many more ahead!) *"Să trăiești, mulți ani!"* (May you live long!)	In Romania, this is used for name days as well (important Christian names such as Vasile, Ioan, Maria, Ilie, Constantin, Elena, Nicolae, etc.) are celebrated and good wishes are expressed.
News about children (when age comes up)		*"Să vă trăiască!"* (Long may he live for you!) *"Mulți înainte!"* (Many more years ahead!)	In Romania, conversation about a child's age immediately triggers this standard phrase
Death, burial, and mourning	*"Herzliches Beileid"* (My sincere condolences)	*"Condoleanțe!"* (My condolences) *"Dumnezeu să îl/o odihnească"* (May God rest his/her soul),	Romania: reference to the eternal peace of the deceased and

Situation	GERMAN	ROMANIAN	Notes
	"Ruhe in Frieden" (Rest in peace)	*"Dumnezeu să îl/o ierte!"* (May God forgive him/her)	forgiveness by God.
Christmas and New Year	*"Frohe Weihnachten!"* (Merry Christmas), *"Schöne/Frohe Festtage/Feiertage!"* (Happy/Beautiful holidays) *"Ein frohes neues Jahr!"* (A Happy New Year!"), *"Einen guten Rutsch ins neue Jahr!"* (Good sliding into the New Year!)	*"Crăciun fericit!"* (Merry Christmas), *"Sărbători fericite!"* (Happy holidays), *"Christos s-a născut!"* (Christ is born! = less common nowadays) *"An Nou fericit!"* (Happy New Year), *"La mulți ani!"* (Many more years)	
Before Easter	*"Frohe Ostern!"* (Happy Easter), *"Schöne/Frohe Festtage/Feiertage!"* (Happy/beautiful holidays)	*"Paște fericit!"* (Happy Easter!), *"Sărbători fericite de Sfintele Paști!"* (Happy holidays for the Holy Easter)	
During and after Easter	*"Frohe Ostern!"* (during)	*"Christos a înviat!"* (Christ has risen from the dead!) -	This greeting and answer can be used 40 days until

Situation	GERMAN	ROMANIAN	Notes
		"Adevărat a înviat!" (In truth He has risen!)	Ascension, but in urban areas, it is used only during the first week after Easter.
When toasting	*"Prost!"* (Cheers!) *"Zum Wohl!* (To your health!)	*"Noroc!"* (Cheers/ ...Good luck!), *"Sănătate!"* (...Good health!), *"Doamne ajută!"* (May the Lord help!), *"Să trăim!"* (May we live!)	RO: a larger variety of wishes when toasting and drinking. Toasting only with alcohol
When sneezing	*"Gesundheit!"* (lit., Health! = bless you)	*"Noroc!"* (Good luck!), *"Sănătate!"* (Health)	
When surprised (bad news), irritated	*"Um Gottes Willen!"* (For God's sake!)	*"Doamne!"* (Lord!), *"Doamne ferește!"* (when thinking about something bad or dangerous = God forbid/May the Lord spare us), *"Doamne iartă-mă!"* (Forgive me, Lord)	*"Doamne ferește"* is very common in Romanian - when faced with bad news, bad prospects, strange ideas.
Before difficult time (exam,	*"Viel Glück!"* (Lots of luck!), *"Viel Erfolg!"* (Lots of success), *"Hals- und Beinbruch!"* (Break a	*"Doamne ajută!"* (May the Lord help!), *"Să dea Dumnezeu să fie bine!"* (May the Lord will it to go	The typical wish before an exam in Romania is *"baftă!"* and the set answer is *"Să*

Situation	GERMAN	ROMANIAN	Notes
operation, journey ahead, etc.)	leg!), *"Gottes segen"* (God's blessing)	well), *"Succes!"* (success), *"Baftă!"* (Good luck!)	*fie!*" (Amen, let there be). There is a superstition that answering *"Mulțumesc"* (Thank you) instead will bring bad luck.
Welcome	*"(Herzlich) Wilkommen"* (Welcome) - Answer: *"Danke"* (Thank you)	*"Bun venit"* (Welcome), *"Bine ați venit/sosit"* (Well have you come/arrived = conjugated) - Answer: *"Bine v-am găsit"* (Well found /Well have we found you)	In Romanian, this is a more complex exchange, in the spirit of hospitality.
Thanking	*"Danke (schön)"/"Vielen/Herzlichen Dank"* – „*Bitte*" or the friendlier „*Gern(e) geschehen*"	*"Mulțumesc (frumos/din suflet/din toată inima)"* – „*Cu plăcere*" (my pleasure) or, more recently, „*Cu drag*" (with love)	Romanians tend to thank less often (very little interaction with the supermarket cashier, for instance), but they do tend to thank

Situation	GERMAN	ROMANIAN	Notes
			profusely when grateful.
Ending phrase for letters	*"Mit freundlichen Grüßen"* (With friendly/polite greetings) - standard and formal *"Viele/Schöne Grüße"* (Many/Kind greetings), *"Herzliche Grüße"* (Sincere/heartfelt greetings) - less formal *"Liebe Grüße"* (with loving/kind greetings) – the least formal	*"Cu deosebită stimă"* (With outstanding respect) = most formal *"Cu stimă/respect"* , *"Cu mulțumiri (pentru solicitudine)"* (With respect, With many thanks (for your solicitousness) = formal *"Cu cordialitate/cu prietenie"* (With cordial friendship) = less formal, but very polite *"Cu drag"* (With love) = very informal.	

Table 17. A brief overview of German and Romanian set phrases and wishes (most common)

The conclusion one can draw is that both languages (and cultures) have a set of standardized phrases for everyday situations and special occasions. As expected from a person-oriented society, Romania has more diverse phrases, more emotional and more intimate wishes for special and religious occasions, for welcoming people and expressing joyous participation in their good news. In Romania, the religious element is more present in everyday speech (this also holds true for Catholic Bavaria). After Easter, Romanians still actually greet each other with "Christ is risen!" and answer "In truth, He is risen!"

Generally speaking, the Germans are more low-key. They appear to be more formal and ceremonious in everyday life (a lot more *please* and *thank you* than Romanians), but less creative and more distant in terms of special wishes for special occasions in other people's lives (basically, limited variations around *Glückwunsch*). To Romanians, this politeness often seems robotic (forced smiles for customers, for instance); while in Germany too much smiling and touching is seen as strange/improper/unprofessional.

Romanians, on the other hand, are much more exuberant when faced with special occasions, but less formal in their day-to-day interactions (less please and thank you). Even their deference (which may appear exaggerated when translated) generates a feeling of familiarity.

To end this section on a more humorous note, the following table aptly illustrates the difference between the practicality and efficiency of German set phrases and the variety and adaptability of Romanian ones:

Bitte	Please	Vă rog / Te rog
Bitte	There you are	Poftiți / Poftim

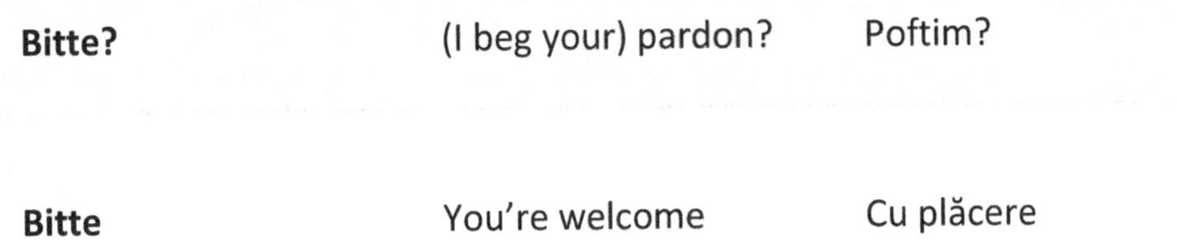

Bitte?	(I beg your) pardon?	Poftim?
Bitte	You're welcome	Cu plăcere

Table 18. Saying please: A comparison between German and Romanian

German small talk is usually limited to a safe zone of discussing the weather, vacation destinations, job, sport/hobbies, and other neutral topics. By contrast, Romanian small talk may also include recent events and personal experiences (even triggering ones!), common acquaintances, family, children, work, health, vacation plans, food and cooking, mild political subjects, etc. There is a considerably larger degree of political correctness and self-censorship in German conversations than in Romanian ones. Romanians open up quite easily about family, current affairs, political views, personal circumstances.

4.4. Beware: profanity ahead! German vs. Romanian humor and curses

4.4.1. German vs. Romanian humor and jokes

Ever since Mark Twain, it has been a cliché among expats that Germans are not very funny. They don't laugh much and don't make foreigners laugh much either. Germans take many things very seriously (too seriously, according to Romanians), thoroughly and often literally. Romanians also think Germans do not understand the double meaning, cannot read between the lines and 'catch a drift', and need explanations for jokes. There might be some truth to this since Germans are indeed not used to indirect and implicit communication. Their virtues - efficiency, competence, and dry sensibleness - seem quite incompatible with humor. A 2011 survey published by the German daily *Die Welt* has the Germans ranking last (15 out of 15 investigated nations) in terms of how humorous they are perceived to be by other nations. Apparently, Germans cannot make others laugh[127].

A German writer and public speaker, Eva Ullmann, even went as far as to establish a German Institute for Humor (www.humorinstitut.de) in Leipzig, with the declared goal of teaching Germans how to deal with stress and conflict by incorporating more humor in their corporate environment.

The reality is that Germans do have humor, it simply is different from that of the English-speaking or Romance-language countries and hard to translate due to language specificity. Some German humor is of rather low, childish quality, but Germany also has a tradition of elevated and searing political cabaret, satire, and parody. Late-night comedy shows on German TV and jokes on Social Media are getting bolder, subtler, and entail self-irony, allusions, and puns. There is political correctness in society that scowls at certain types of jokes that are too daring or reminiscent of the Nazi era, and Germans will refrain from laughing at jokes they perceive as discriminatory (inner inhibitions through education). They also do not normally appreciate vulgar jokes (at least not in public).

---

[127] Die Welt, "Die Deutschen sind die unwitzigste Nation", http://www.welt.de/kultur/article13421700/Die-Deutschen-sind-die-unwitzigste-Nation.html, 06.04.2016

Germans laugh about mishaps and embarrassing situations (happening to others, laugh less at themselves), about other nations (especially Austrians, Dutch, Swiss, fellow Germans (Ostfriesen, Swabians, Bavarians), about state officials, about the not so stupid boy *Fritzchen*, about dull machos who drive Opel Mantas, farmers. There are also "*kommt ein...*" jokes (someone comes to someone else, dialog ensues), and 'anti-jokes' (short, absurd jokes without a punch line), puns, Carnival speeches, stand-up comedy, and cabaret. Sharp social and political satire (including using irony) is growing in quality and frequency (see Die Heute Show, X 3, the recent satire against Erdogan, etc.).

Romanians have a tradition of laughing their troubles away and laughing in the face of destiny. (For instance, one of the last jokes of the poverty-stricken Ceausescu era was: "*How do you castrate a refrigerator? By taking the last two eggs out of it!*" [128]). They can laugh at almost everything and mock almost everyone, including themselves. They even have special terms for this type of funny mockery, such as *mișto*, or *bășcălie*. These refer to not taking things seriously, pulling someone's leg, making fun of perceived weaknesses, deriding everything.

Romanian humor is based a lot on double meanings, hidden meanings, situational humor, irony, and self-irony (although recently, comedians deplore that the willingness of Romanians to accept self-irony has decreased, as has the quality of TV shows[129]).

---

[128] Ştefănescu, C. B., *Umorul poporului român în faza terminală a socialismului*, Paideia, Bucureşti, 2014, p. 78
[129] Ionescu, S. in Adevărul, "Cum se fac glumele şi de cine mai râd românii", http://adevarul.ro/locale/constanta/cum-fac-glumele-mai-rad-romanii-secretele-marilor-umoristi-dragos-patraru-patriarhul-suna-disperare-tvr-scoata-emisiunea-

Romanians like to joke when they hang out, when they meet friends, or at work. They believe stressful, tedious, or repetitive tasks can be made easier and more pleasant by a little harmless fun. They often share jokes online, like to make witty remarks in conversation (though less so than the Americans). There are countless online databases of jokes, as well as online newspapers exclusively for jokes (TimesNewRoman, Kamikaze), almanacs with jokes, etc. Romanians laugh at themselves, at Romanians from other regions (*ardeleni, olteni, moldoveni*), at other nations. Romanian jokes can often be "without curtains" (irreverent, to downright vulgar and obscene). Except for God (and by extension, the Church), there are no politically correct taboos - and in many circles, priests and the Church are fair game as well.

Romanian jokes include jokes about their national flaws, about Americans/ Russians / Hungarians / Jews / Scots / Brits, about communism/socialism, about Nazis, about politicians, national habits, about starvation in Somalia, about policemen, about the President, dark humor, British humor, *Bulă* jokes (*Bulă* is a type of Fritzchen, uneducated, promiscuous, but often street smart and with a lot of gall), *Dorel* jokes (*Dorel* is the archetype of the incompetent handyman /construction worker), sadistic jokes (*Alinuța* jokes), dirty and lewd jokes (*bancuri "deocheate"*), sexual innuendo, jokes about blondes, jokes about politicians, jokes about Radio Yerevan, jokes about iconic macho characters (Chuck Norris).

Political pamphlets, sitcoms, parodies, political cabaret also abound on all TV stations, ranging from low-quality to subtle. In fact, during the communist

---

1 56fe261e5ab6550cb874af60/index.html, 09.04.2016

dictatorship, subtlety was a potentially life-saving prerequisite. Romanians vented frustration and laughed at the regime using very indirect secret and highly contextual jokes, allusions that the censorship couldn't catch, but which the audience understood (these were called *şopârle* = "lizards").

The following is an example of a joke in which Romanians poke fun at their stereotypes:

(At a Romanian construction site:)

- Boss, my shovel just broke! What should I do?

- Well, lean on the cement mixer from now on, we're out of shovels!

This joke requires context about Romanian frustration with how slowly new infrastructure projects are being built. It not only pokes fun at the lazy individual, but at an entire system and pattern of behavior - since they are out of shovels, it means all construction workers have broken theirs - not from too much work, but from too much leaning on them.

The next joke is an example of a Romanian joke which, again, pokes fun at Romanian issues (bad roads), but also involves Germans - portrayed here in their stereotype as car connoisseurs, people who know quality when they see it:

(At a car dealership:)

Two Germans conversing:

- What's this? The Dacia Duster?

- Duster, yes, it appears to be a car...

- Romanian, right?

- Yes, I believe it is Romanian.

- Looks good, doesn't it? High road clearance, broad tires, four-wheel drive...

- Yeah... I'll tell you, these darned Romanians! They would do anything to avoid fixing their roads!

4.4.2. Parental Guidance! German vs. Romanian curses and insults

Germans are polite, reserved, and conscientious. They refrain from showing emotions in public, and there is an even greater taboo on showing negative emotions. Insulting someone outside of a comedy setting is almost unthinkable. German has relatively few curse words or expletives, and the most common ones are impersonal: *Scheiße* (most common, shit), *Mist* (manure). Another very innocent way to show frustration is *Verflixt* (Shoot!, Darn!). There are the occasional damnings and curses involving the devil ("*Was zum Teufel*" = what the hell, *Scher dich zum Teufel* = go to hell) and some connected to sex organs (*Verpiss dich!* = Piss off!, *Leck mich am Arsch* = Kiss my ass). Some of the curses and insults directed at people are *depp* (fool), *bekloppt* (insane, cuckoo), *bescheuert* (crackbrained), *Vollidiot* (complete idiot), *Arschloch* (asshole), *Blöde Kuh* (stupid cow – for women), *Dreckskerl/Drecksau* (filthy swine, dirty skunk, son of a bitch), *Vollpfosten* (dumbass). So one can conclude the most common German insults have to do with dirtiness/defecation and stupidity/ineptitude.

Romanian curses and insults can appear quite intense, vulgar, and obscene by comparison. Romanians curse and talk lewdly a lot, even in public (through the centuries, this has established itself as a way of venting accumulated frustration), or even for a good laugh, as a way of filling the gaps and 'peppering' one's conversation. There is an enormous quantity and variety of curses and insults in Romanian. The most common exclamations include damnings (*Ce naiba!, La dracu!*), or have to do with the devil and his mother (such as: go to the devil, may the devil take you, you devil's fool, when I'm finished with you the devil's mother will take you). Others yet have to do with sending someone back to the origins (*du-te-n p... mătii* – go back into your mother's vagina), with female reproduction organs, with the male sexual organ, vulgar sexual terminology, and oral sex, but "shit" (*rahat*) is also very common. There are also numerous insults such as idiot, dumb animal, ox, cretin, ant-brain, peasant, etc. This is in line with the more emotional nature of Romanians, and the lack of strong taboos on outbursts of emotions. In most cases, verbal violence helps defuse inner tensions (short-lived emotional discharge) and so, despite all this dirty talk and verbal violence, the level of socio-political violence in Romania is quite low.

4.5. German vs. Romanian communication styles, practices, and competences

Apart from personal experience and informal interviews with participants in both cultures, I rely heavily on R.D. Lewis (2008) to identify and summarize cultural traits that affect business communication in Germany and Romania.

Please see the following pages for more insights.

COMMUNICATION PATTERNS AT MEETINGS[130]	GERMANY	ROMANIA
	<ul><li>Start (punctual)</li><li>Short introduction (brief warm-up, small talk, ice-breaker)</li><li>Contents (full background information, circumstances, topics and goals of meeting; serious style, weighty work climate)</li><li>Getting into the subject : Proposal and Counterarguments (directness, frankness, honesty; logic and specific)</li><li>Determining the solution (seeking common ground)</li><li>Agreeing on a solution, putting control measures in place, clarity</li><li>Conclusions and follow-up</li></ul>	<ul><li>Delays likely, preamble often long-winded, oratorical</li><li>Proposal (delicate)</li><li>Listening to counter-proposal without abandoning their own</li><li>Skepticism ("that won't work in Romania", hints, indirect clues)</li><li>Negotiation (imaginative, answers questions with questions, may say what you want to hear, sophistication in discourse, no simple answers, flexible truth)</li><li>Haggling (can be time-consuming, unpredictable, seek personal rather than organizational support)</li><li>Agreement (possibly ambiguous)</li></ul>

	GERMANY	ROMANIA
LISTENING HABITS[131]	<ul><li>Germans are good, disciplined listeners, often poker-faced</li><li>Germans expect plenty of background, detailed information, repetition, and seriousness</li><li>Germans are used to complex and heavy messages</li><li>Germans will ask concrete questions and want to know what it costs</li></ul>	<ul><li>Romanians are attentive but suspicious listeners</li><li>They may interrupt when they disagree</li><li>They expect to be treated as equals and can see through simplistic arguments</li><li>Hyperbole and charisma are OK, but they do not like: being talked down to, official pomposity, or ideology</li><li>Quick, often lengthy feedback; quite often, their message structure is non-linear, back-and-forth, a mix of factual and personal arguments.</li></ul>

---

[130] Lewis, R.D., *Cross-Cultural Communication: A Visual Approach*, Transcreen Publications, Warnford, 2008, pp. 6-7 and 22-23

[131] Lewis, R.D., *Cross-Cultural Communication: A Visual Approach*, Transcreen Publications, Warnford, 2008, pp. 64-65 and 80-81

	GERMANY	ROMANIA
AUDIENCE EXPECTATIONS DURING PRESENTATIONS[132]	• solid company • solid product • technical information • background and context • clear structure, serious attitude, tidy appearance • lots of text, few or no jokes • good price • quality • delivery date	• make them feel special, unique, worth your while • sophistication of discourse, versatility, rhetorical skill, and charismatic delivery • logical arguments • flexible truth • well-dressed speakers • delicacy and indirectness • no more ideologies
LANGUAGE OF MANAGEMENT[133]	• formal • data-oriented, task-oriented, detailed • clear orders, supervision • hierarchical but team-oriented (seeking a certain degree of consensus)	• expressive, rich language which forms a strong bond • broad possibilities of expressing nuances, ambiguous language • some emotional manipulation, some cynicism, and pragmatism, some paternalism

Table 19. Germany vs. Romania - A brief comparison of communication styles in business settings (adapted from R.D. Lewis, *Cross-Cultural Communication: A Visual Approach*, 2008).

---

[132] idem, pp. 119 and 123
[133] ibidem, pp. 198-199, 214-215.

On a lighter, funnier note, this diagram represents very aptly the post-communist skepticism and negativity of Romanians in communication (especially amongst themselves):

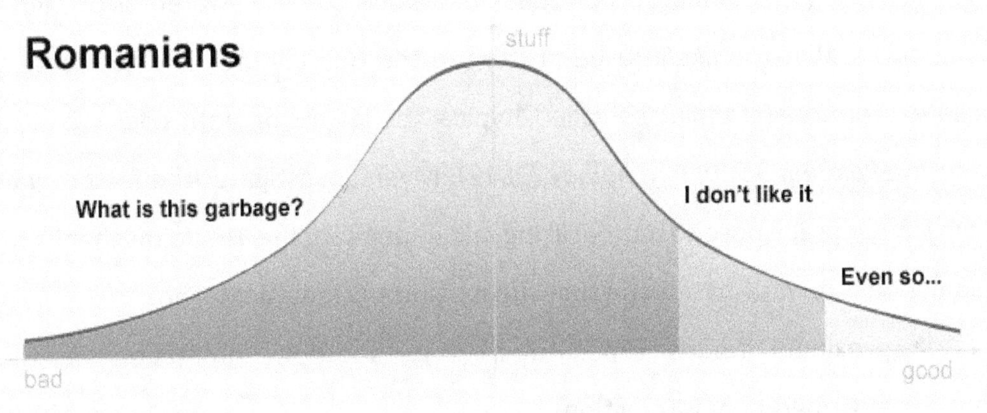

Source: Costache, O. on Medium.com blog, https://medium.com/octavians-thoughts/what-does-its-a-good-start-really-mean-ff8c1a2495c4#.n9aij5qp2, accessed on 06.04.2016

5. Making Sense of It All: Practical Suggestions. Communicating Effectively and Finding Common Ground

As already mentioned in the introduction, this book does not intend to generate preconceived ideas or fixed expectations that end up creating their own realities (self-fulfilling prophecies), but rather to raise awareness of values and norms that *are likely* to be present in the two cultures and to create a context for understanding so-called "typical" behaviors on both sides.

In *Exploring Social Psychology (2012),* Myers investigates the factors that can lead or predispose to mutual liking and understanding. He claims that liking someone is reward-based and that the most important factors are:[134]

- ❖ proximity (mere exposure to one another, interaction or the anticipation of interaction),
- ❖ attractiveness (being well-dressed, looking your best for the encounter),
- ❖ matching the counterpart (we like those who like us), and
- ❖ similarity.

In brief, that which you already know or are often exposed to, you will tend to like more. The purpose of this book was to identify and investigate those areas of both similarity and complementarity to bring the sides closer to each other and familiarize them with otherness.

There has been extensive and very interesting research on intra-group and inter-group dynamics, and one fascinating result is that group-think and

---

[134] Myers, D.G., *Exploring Social Psychology (6th edition),* McGraw-Hill, New York, 2012, pp. 315-332

categorical thinking can often lead to a so-called 'ultimate attribution error' (Pettigrew, 1979), whereby people tend to be more lenient with individuals from their own group, and a lot tougher on outsiders. Bad behavior within one's in-group is often explained away as being caused by external circumstances, while bad behavior from the other group is attributed to some inherent trait or genetic disposition of 'those people'. What's more, the opposite is true for good behavior. Positive ingroup behavior is attributed to inherent traits (that's just the way we are), while positive outgroup behavior is seen as a fluke, or attributed to luck, special circumstances, individual high motivation. In the words of Plous (2003), "this attributional double standard makes it virtually impossible for outgroup members to break free of prejudice against them because their positive actions are explained away while their failures and shortcomings are used against them."[135]

According to Schulz von Thun (1981), all communication includes four different aspects (the four sides, functions, or purposes of the message): an objective, *factual* side (pure information), a *self-revelation* side (conveys something personal about the speaker), a phatic or *relationship-building* side (communicates something about the relationship speaker-receiver or attempts to build a relationship), and a *persuasive* side (imperative, makes an appeal, attempts to influence). Different interpretations of the same message (depending on which "ear" is used to absorb it – in other words, whether the recipient hears with their factual/phatic/self-revelation/appeal ears) can lead

---

[135] Plous, S., *Understanding Prejudice and Discrimination, McGraw-Hill*, New York, 2003, p. 16

to misunderstandings and conflict. Paul Watzlawick postulated that each message can be understood in terms of content or relationship.

To put it simplistically, it would appear that Germans (at least in an organizational context) are more focused on the factual content, the informational side, while Romanians are more open to (and eager for) the relationship and self-revelation sides of the message box.

Based on our research so far[136], it is fairly likely that Romanians would get more out of their interactions with Germans if they:

- understand the German need for structure, order, and rationality
- come well-prepared with facts, details, numbers, dates, rational arguments, and counterarguments; show how they reached their conclusions; think ahead for the long haul and use a more cohesive, more linear argumentation structure, building on things in logical order and clarifying one aspect before jumping to the next
- are punctual and well-dressed, polite and self-confident
- discuss all aspects patiently, calmly, and professionally; there is no going back on a done deal
- try to remain objective, keep it cool and refrain from taking things personally when the Germans appear too blunt or critical
- adopt more cooperative, integrative communication patterns[137]
- limit their emotional outbursts and interruptions, avoid embarrassing the Germans

---

[136] see also Lewis (2004, 2008)

[137] see Paul Grice's four maxims of the Cooperative Principle, in "Logic and Conversation." Pp. 41–58 in Syntax and Semantics 3: Speech Acts, edited by P. Cole and J. J. Morgan. New York, NY: Academic Press.

- do not introduce humor and avoid irreverent jokes; are not nosy, pushy, or indiscreet

- keep their need for closeness and personal liking in check, do not rely too much on subjectivity

- understand that Germans do not strike deals based on personal likes or dislikes (it is not enough to convince only the person in front of you), use deliberate and solid arguments that stand up to scrutiny and convince an entire organization

- have patience for longer explanations and procedures on the German side (Germans like thoroughness and consensus as a prerequisite for steady future commitment)

- make notes, be prepared to put everything in writing, and check their terms carefully

- complete action chains, are honest and reliable, show the Germans that they have self-control and can be their equal

- understand and accept that clear rules, procedures, accountability, and professionalism are essential for delivering consistent quality and for long-term success.

On the other hand, Germans could empathize with Romanians better if they:

- come prepared for more human contact, more closeness, bigger gestures, and ready to open up a little on a personal level

- come prepared for longer kick-off and probing phases, with relationship-building (over food and drinks), possible delays (15-30 minutes late is considered polite for private visits at home), and changes of plan

- pay attention to body language, looks, non-verbal and indirect clues; do not assume you know the whole story even when things appear cut and dried

- show interest and do not talk down to Romanians, do not start criticizing their society right away, appreciate Romanian hospitality (Romanians put a lot of effort into treating guests well)

- are more tactful and diplomatic: a little compliment about Romanians or Romania can go a long way

- understand that Romanians prefer to like and get along with the person they are dealing with (a good, smooth personal relationship is just as important as good services and metrics, because Romanians think, 'We will manage the metrics somehow, but I will have to deal with this person every day.')

- show some flexibility and sophistication beyond the dry details of the procedure or the bottom line, try to enjoy themselves too, but avoid getting so chummy that they lose authority

- let Romanians talk and digress, be prepared to explore new ideas that were not on the initial agenda, be aware of hyperbolic, emotional language, and understand the Romanian need for self-revelation and personal connection

- are prepared for several people talking at once, for interruptions and intense emotions.

Returning to our initial anecdote, the German pharmacists were simply going about their business in the sequential (monochronic) fashion so typical of their culture, in a structured, rational, and thorough way, following procedure and giving their undivided attention to the current customer. An interruption to say "Hi" might have been interpreted as rude by that customer, and it might have affected the shop assistant's focus or the privacy of the sales conversation. At work, the German is inseparable from his role and does not sell on his personality, but rather on the quality and objective characteristics of the product or service provided. The Romanian customer would have liked a friendlier and more flexible attitude, a validating greeting, an accommodating interest in her particular situation, less distance, and faster multitasking.

These findings notwithstanding, it is the author's deepest belief that the true foundation of improved mutual understanding rests on three pillars: open-mindedness, authenticity, and mutual respect.

One has to understand that, with investigating culture, there is always a trade-off between completeness (accuracy) and timeliness. By the time research studies are published and the academic literature is read, gradual but significant cultural shifts might have already happened. Whatever the textbook cases might suggest, real interactions happen between real people, individuals that might or might not be representative of 'their culture'. The potential for positive surprises, but also for misunderstandings and conflicts is never really exhausted. Humans are influenced by their genes, their environment, even their level of sleep deprivation, hunger, or the weather outside. Do not jump to conclusions. Do not try to immediately assign people to a predetermined box.

Cooperation between Germans and Romanians is not only possible, but it has proven very lucrative. In 2013, Germany was Romania's largest trade partner, with imports from Germany amounting to EUR 11.2 bln, and Romanian exports to Germany adding up to a total of EUR 10.1 bln.[138] And the trend continued. According to Statista, by 2020 Germany had retained and even widened its lead as Romania's largest trade partner, exports from Romania to Germany totaling EUR 14.1 bln that year alone.[139]

Overwhelmingly, Romanian immigrants to Germany adjust better and are better integrated into the labor market than other nationalities[140], possibly due to their non-confrontational streak, their networking and survival skills, their education, and creativity.

Combined with German thoroughness, Romanian creativity can lead to extraordinary results. German order and rigor, an efficient German system of management, fair rewards, good career prospects, and an environment that allows for the Romanian need for warmth and close relationships can help Romanians reach their full potential and deliver high-quality products and services. Complementarities can generate synergies.

Over the past 30 years, Romania has experienced a dramatic brain drain and is currently going through a tense reevaluation of its cultural and socio-political paradigms. Media competence is not at its highest in Romania, neither

---

[138] Vocea Timişului, online edition, "Germania rămâne cel mai important partener comercial al României", http://voceatimisului.ro/germania-ramane-cel-mai-important-partener-comercial-al-romaniei, 02.04.2015

[139] See https://www.statista.com/statistics/1094615/export-partner-countries-romania/, 02.2022

[140] Bundesagentur für Arbeit, Institut für Arbeitsmarkt und Berufsforschung (IAB), "Zuwanderungsmonitor Bulgarien und Rumänien", online edition, http://doku.iab.de/arbeitsmarktdaten/Zuwanderungsmonitor_1501.pdf, (published 01.2015)

is science education anymore. Polarization has increased, as has inequality, and is likely to increase further in the future, with educated urban elites increasingly adopting a Western lifestyle focused on good governance, transparency, flat hierarchies, and technological progress, while many rural areas are paternalistic and conservative, jobless, depopulated, and left behind. It will be interesting to observe which way the pendulum will finally swing, especially given the combined dilemmas raised by the Covid-19 pandemic, social media, new work, big data, and climate change.

Given their recent history, Romanians are trained to deal with adversity, to improvise and make do with less, to create supportive networks, and to connect with people on a more intimate level. In the words of Adrienne Rubatos, they "muddle through with a shrewdness born of necessity"[141]. This can benefit Germans as well, helping them think outside the box and 'keep their ear to the ground'. German investments can raise the Romanian living standards and thus convince Romanians of the benefits of carrying things through and getting consistent results. And Romanian emotionality, hospitality, person-orientation, and love of traditions can enrich the German experience and outlook on life.

---

[141] Rubatos, A., diversophy.com, http://diversophy.com/collections/europe/products/romania, 06.04.2016

Bibliography

Alexe, Dan (2015). Dacopatia și alte rătăciri românești. București: Humanitas

Allport, G. W. (1954). The nature of prejudice. Cambridge, MA: Perseus Books

Anonymous, online collection of German jokes (2016). http://www.spitzenwitze.de/

Anonymous, online collection of Romanian jokes (2016). www.bancuri.net

Autobild (2012). "Zeit zum Abspecken",

http://www.autobild.de/artikel/fahrzeuggewicht-frueher-und-heute-1268731.html

BlastingNews (2015). "Rumänen und Bulgaren, Sozialschmarotzer oder deutscher

Wirtschaftsmotor", http://de.blastingnews.com/politik/2015/06/rumanen-und-

bulgaren-sozialschmarotzer-oder-deutscher-wirtschaftsmotor-00423879.html

Boia, Lucian (2012). De ce este România altfel? București: Humanitas

Botezatu and Hâncu (2001). Dicționar de proverbe și zicători românești. București:

Brücker, H., Hauptmann, A., Vallizadeh, E. - Bundesagentur für Arbeit (2015).

"Zuwanderungsmonitor Bulgarien und Rumänien". Nürnberg: Institut für

Arbeitsmarkt- und Berufsforschung.

Bundestag (2016). ,

http://www.bundestag.de/bundestag/wahlen/ergebnisse_seit1949/244692

Business Insider Deutschland (2016). "Aus Deutschland kommen mehr gefährliche

Produkte als aus China — und hier sind einige davon",

http://www.businessinsider.de/gefaehrliche-produkte-aus-deutschland-2016-

4?utm_source=yahoode&utm_medium=referral&ref=yfp

Cărtărescu, M. (2010). Frumoasele străine. București: Humanitas

Children's Society (2015). "The Good Childhood Report 2015".

David, Daniel (2015). Psihologia poporului român. București: Polirom

DerWeg.org (2016). https://www.derweg.org/deutschland/geschichte/

Detektor.fm (2015). "Das Märchen vom faulen Ausländer",

http://detektor.fm/gesellschaft/studienien-migration-aus-bulgarien-und-rumaenien

Die Welt (2013). "Heikles Selbstbild - Die Rumänen und ihr Gefühl, wertlos zu sein", online edition, http://www.welt.de/debatte/kommentare/article113852181/Die-Rumaenen-und-ihr-Gefuehl-wertlos-zu-sein.html and (2011). "Die Deutschen sind die unwitzigste Nation", http://www.welt.de/kultur/article13421700/Die-Deutschen-sind-die-unwitzigste-Nation.html

Die Zeit (2014). "Wie ein Bürger dritter Klasse", http://www.zeit.de/gesellschaft/2014-01/integration-deutschland-rumaenien

Digi24 (2015). "A crescut încrederea românilor în Președinție și a scăzut încrederea în Biserică",http://www.digi24.ro/Stiri/Digi24/Actualitate/Social/INSCOP+A+scazut+incredurea+in+Biserica

Djuvara, N. (2008). O scurtă istorie a românilor povestită celor tineri. București: Humanitas

Duden (2014). Sprichwörter und Redewendungen aus aller Welt. Berlin: Dudenverlag

Europa Liberă România (2023). "Recensământ 2022. De ce este religia marea necunoscută, cu 15% dintre români nedeclarați", https://romania.europalibera.org/a/religie-recensamant2022-romani-/32210549.html

Florian, C. M. (2012). Zweieinhalb Störche: Roman einer Kindheit in Siebenbürgen. Berlin: Transit Buchverlag

Frankfurter Neue Presse (2016). "Wie falsch Vorurteile gegen Rumänen sind - Intoleranz und billiges Gemüse", http://www.fnp.de/rhein-main/dasprojektjungezeitung/Intoleranz-und-billiges-Gemuese;art11422,1851082

Fromkin, V. et al. (2014). An Introduction to Language. USA: Wadsworth

GfK Nurnberg e.V. (2006). "Was ist deutsch?" http://www.nbaservice.com/europa_image_deutschland.html

Grice, P. (1975). "Logic and Conversation." Pp. 41–58 in Syntax and Semantics 3: Speech Acts, edited by P. Cole and J. J. Morgan. New York, NY: Academic Press

Grimm, W., Grimm, J. (2009). Grimms Märchen. Vollständige Ausgabe. Deutschland: Null-Papier Verlag - http://www.grimmstories.com/de/grimm_maerchen/index

Hall, E.T. (1976). Beyond Culture. New York: Anchor Books

Hall, E.T & Reed Hall, M. (1990). Understanding Cultural Differences. Yarmouth: Intercultural Press

Hedeșan, O., Mușat N., Percec, D., Popa, C., Rus, C. (2011). Manual de orientare culturală pentru străini. Timișoara: Mirton.

Hofstede, G, Hofstede G.J., Minkov, M. (2010). Cultures and Organizations. Software of the Mind. Revised and expanded 3rd edition. New York: McGraw-Hill

Hofstede, G. (1997). Cultures and Organizations. Software of the Mind. Intercultural Cooperation and Its Importance for Survival. 2nd edition. New York: McGraw-Hill

Inglehart and Welzel (2015). "The WVS Cultural Map of the World", http://www.worldvaluessurvey.org

INSCOP (2016). "Barometrul Adevărul despre România". București: http://www.inscop.ro/barometrul-inscop-adevarul-despre-romania-2/

Ispirescu, P., Creangă, I. et. al (1984). Basmele românilor. București: Ed. Ion Creangă

Ispirescu, P. (1975). Märchen. Berlin: Altberliner Verlag

Kluckhohn, F.R., Strodtbeck, F.L. (1961). Variations in Value Orientations.

Kumbier, D., Schulz von Thun, F. (2006). Interkulturelle Kommunikation: Methoden, Modelle, Beispiele. Rowohlt-Taschenbuch-Verlag

Lassiter, G.D. et al., (2005). "Attributional Complexity and the Camera Perspective Bias in Videotaped Confessions" in Basic and Applied Psychology, 27(1)

Lewicki, R.J., Barry, B., Saunders, D.M. (2020). Negotiation. New York: McGraw Hill

Lewis, R.D. (2004). When Cultures Collide. Managing Successfully Across Cultures. London: Nicholas Brealy Publishing

Lewis, R.D. (2008). Cross-Cultural Communication: A Visual Approach. Warnford: Transcreen Publications

Liiceanu, G. (2010). Întâlnire cu un necunoscut. București: Humanitas

Lizard, T.W., Gheorghiu O. C. (2014) How to survive Romania. Bucharest: Lizard&Partners

Luca, Adina (2005). "A Study on the Position of Romania on Hofstede's Cultural Dimensions". Bucharest: Interact Consulting

Manpower Group Deutschland (2014). "MPG_Infografik_Jobmotivation.pdf, Top 10 Faktoren der Jobmotivation"

Mediafax (2015). "Deficitul balanței comerciale a urcat cu 15% în S1", http://www.mediafax.ro/economic/deficitul-balantei-comerciale-a-urcat-cu-15-in-s1-importuri-30-miliarde-euro-exporturi-27-miliarde-euro-14670007 and "România, pe ultimul loc în Europa după numărul de IMM-uri active", http://www.mediafax.ro/economic/romania-pe-ultimul-loc-in-europa-dupa-numarul-de-imm-uri-active-13773363

Medium.com (2012). https://medium.com/octavians-thoughts/what-does-its-a-good-start-really-mean-ff8c1a2495c4#.n9aij5qp2

Meyer, E. (2014). The Culture Map. New York: Public Affairs

McCurdy, D. W., Spradley, J., Shandy, D. J. (2005). The Cultural Experience - Ethnography in Complex Society. Long Grove: Waveland Press.

Mietwagen-Auskunft.de (2016). http://www.mietwagen-auskunft.de/rumaenien/mentalitaet/

Mungiu-Pippidi, A. (2012). De ce nu iau românii Premiul Nobel. București: Polirom

Myers, D.G. (2012). Exploring Social Psychology. New York: McGraw-Hill

Pettigrew, T. F. (1979). "The ultimate attribution error: Extending Allport's cognitive analysis of prejudice" in Personality and Social Psychology Bulletin 5(4)

Pleşu, A.(2006). Despre bucurie în est și în vest. București: Humanitas

Plous, S. (2003). Understanding Prejudice and Discrimination. New York: McGraw-Hill

Pondy, L. R. (1967). "Organizational Conflict: Concepts and Models" in Administrative Science Quarterly 12(2)

Profit.ro (2016). "Femeile câștigă cu 9% mai puțin decât bărbații și sunt hărțuite la muncă. Recomandări pentru firme: munca la domiciliu și day-care pentru copii", http://www.profit.ro/stiri/social/document-femeile-castiga-cu-9-mai-putin-decat-barbatii-si-sunt-hartuite-la-munca-recomandari-pentru-firme-munca-la-domiciliu-si-day-care-pentru-copii-15430957

Rădulescu-Motru, C. (1937/1999). Psihologia poporului român. Bucharest: Paideia

Rădulescu-Motru, C. (1910). Sufletul neamului nostru. Bucharest: A. Baer

Realitatea.net (2015). "Studiu: Cât de mult se uită românii la televizor și ce programe preferă", online edition, http://www.realitatea.net/cat-de-mult-de-uita-romanii-la-televizor-si-ce-programe-prefera_1795074.html

Schulz von Thun, F., Sundmacher, M. (2013). Miteinander reden:1. Berlin: Rowohlt

Spiegel Online (2015). "WWF Studie: Deutsche werfen 313 Kilo Lebensmittel weg - pro Sekunde", http://www.spiegel.de/wissenschaft/natur/wwf-studie-millionen-tonnen-lebensmittel-landen-im-muell-a-1039485.html, and "Gehaltsunterschiede der Geschlechter: Warum Frauen weniger verdienen", http://www.spiegel.de/unispiegel/jobundberuf/gender-pay-gap-warum-bekommen-frauen-weniger-lohn-a-1024229.html

Statistisches Bundesamt. (2014). "Ausländische Bevölkerung nach Zensus und Ausländerzentralregister (AZR)" and (2010). "Die Entwicklung der Kirchenmitglieder in Deutschland"

Ștefănescu, C.-B. (2014). Umorul poporului român în faza terminală a socialismului. Bucharest: Paideia

Thomas, A., Kammhuber, S., Schroll-Machl, S. (2003). Handbuch Interkulturelle Kommunikation und Kooperation. 2 Bände. Göttingen: Vandenhoeck & Ruprecht

Thomas, A., Rubatos, A. (2011). Beruflich in Rumänien. Göttingen: Vandenhoeck & Ruprecht

Transparency International (2016, 2023). Corruption Perception Index 2015, 2022

Trompenaars, F., Hampden-Turner, C. (1998). Riding the Waves of Culture. New York: Nicholas Brealy Publishing

The Times Europe (2015). "Germans begin to recast themselves as victims of the Nazis", http://www.thetimes.co.uk/tto/news/world/europe/article4426313.ece

Tuner, A (2013), "Människors interagerande:normer och värderingar inom svenskhet och hur de speglas av idiomatiska uttryck- Parallella svenska och rumänska världar", https://www.dropbox.com/s/xwy3t86gvaxznej/ARTIKEL_ADINA_FINAL.doc?dl=0

Twain, Mark (2014). A Tramp abroad. Tustin:xlst Publishing.

Tylor, E. B. (1871). Primitive Culture. New York: J. P. Putnam's Sons. Vol. 1

Vocea Timișului (2015). "Germania rămâne cel mai important partener comercial al României", http://voceatimisului.ro/germania-ramane-cel-mai-important-partener-comercial-al-romaniei/

Ziarul Adevărul (2016). "Cum se fac glumele și de cine mai râd românii", http://adevarul.ro/locale/constanta/cum-fac-glumele-mai-rad-romanii-secretele-marilor-umoristi-dragos-patraru-patriarhul-suna-disperare-tvr-scoata-emisiunea-1_56fe261e5ab6550cb874af60/index.html

Ziarul Financiar (2015). "Top campioni la exporturi pe județe", online edition, http://www.zf.ro/companii/in-aproape-o-treime-din-judetele-tarii-cel-mai-mare-exportator-vine-din-industria-auto-14846958

Ziarul Lumina (2010). "Miturile esențiale ale culturii românești, Miorița și Meșterul Manole", http://ziarullumina.ro/miturile-esentiale-ale-culturii-romanesti-miorita-si-mesterul-manole-26054.html

Yule, G. (2014). The Study of Language. Cambridge: Cambridge University Press.

ABOUT THE AUTHOR

Andreea Sepi is a Romanian writer and communication professional with a complex intercultural background and an undying interest in bringing people together. She is based in southern Germany, where she works as a writer, translator, language trainer, marketer, and intercultural consultant.